Microsoft® Word 2016

by Jill Murphy, Custom Performance Solutions

LEVEL 2

LABYRINTH

LEARNING™

Microsoft Word 2016: Level 2

Copyright © 2017 by Labyrinth Learning

Labyrinth Learning
2560 9th Street, Suite 320
Berkeley, California 94710
800.522.9746
On the web at lablearning.com

Product Manager:
Jason Favro

Development Manager:
Laura Popelka

Senior Editor:
Alexandra Mummery

Junior Editor:
Alexandria Henderson

**Assessment and Multimedia
Content Development:**
Ben Linford, Judy Mardar, Andrew
Vaughnley

Production Manager:
Debra Grose

Compositor:
Happenstance Type-O-Rama

Indexer:
Valerie Perry

Interior Design:
Debra Grose

Cover Design:
Mick Koller

Labyrinth Learning™ and the Labyrinth Learning logo are trademarks of Labyrinth Learning. Microsoft® is a registered trademark of Microsoft Corporation in the United States and/or other countries and is used by Labyrinth Learning under license from owner. This title is an independent publication not affiliated with Microsoft Corporation. Other product and company names mentioned herein may be the trademarks of their respective owners.

The example companies, organizations, products, people, and events depicted herein are fictitious. No association with any real company, organization, product, person, or event is intended or should be inferred.

Screenshots reprinted with permission.

ebook only ITEM: 1-59136-839-1
ISBN-13: 978-159136-839-7

ebook with printed textbook ITEM: 1-59136-840-5
ISBN-13: 978-159136-840-3

Manufactured in the United States of America

GPP 10 9 8 7 6 5 4 3 2

Table of Contents

Preface

This textbook is part of our brand-new approach to learning for introductory computer courses. We've kept the best elements of our proven instructional design and added powerful, interactive elements and assessments that offer enormous potential to engage learners in a new way. We're delighted with the results, and we hope that learners and educators are, too!

Why Did We Write This Content?

In today's digital world, knowing how to use the most common software applications is critical, and those who don't are left behind. Our goal is to simplify the entire learning experience and help every student develop the practical, real-world skills needed to be successful at work and in school. Using a combination of text, videos, interactive elements, and assessments, we begin with fundamental concepts and take learners through a systematic progression of exercises to reach mastery.

What Key Themes Did We Follow?

We had conversations with dozens of educators at community colleges, vocational schools, and other learning environments in preparation for this textbook. We listened and have adapted our learning solution to match the needs of a rapidly changing world, keeping the following common themes in mind:

Keep it about skills. Our content focus is on critical, job-ready topics and tasks, with a relentless focus on practical, real-world skills and common sense as well as step-by-step instruction to ensure that learners stay engaged from the first chapter forward. We've retained our proven method of progressively moving learners through increasingly independent exercises to ensure mastery—an approach that has been successfully developing skills for more than 20 years.

Keep it simple. Our integrated solutions create a seamless and engaging experience built on a uniquely dynamic instructional design that brings clarity to even the most challenging topics. We've focused our content on the things that matter most and have presented it in the easiest way for today's learners to absorb it. Concise chunks of text are combined with visually engaging and interactive elements to increase understanding for all types of learners.

Keep it relevant. Fresh, original, and constantly evolving content helps educators keep pace with today's student and work environments. We have reviewed every topic for relevancy and have updated it where needed to offer realistic examples and projects for learners.

How Do I Use This Book?

We understand that we are in a time of transition and that some students will still appreciate a print textbook to support their learning. Our comprehensive learning solution consists of a groundbreaking interactive ebook for primary content delivery and our easy-to-use eLab course management tool for assessment. We want to help students as they transition to a digital solution. Our interactive ebook contains learning content delivered in ways that will engage learners. Students can utilize a print text supplement in conjunction with the ebook that provides all the textual elements from the ebook in a full-color, spiral-bound print format.

Our eLab platform provides additional learning content such as overviews for each chapter, automatically graded projects and other assessments that accurately assess student skills, and clear feedback and analytics on student actions.

Included with Your Textbook Purchase

▶ *Interactive ebook*: A dynamic, engaging, and truly interactive textbook that includes elements such as videos, self-assessments, slide shows, and other interactive features. Highlighting, taking notes, and searching for content is easy.

▶ *eLab Course Management System*: A robust tool for accurate assessment, tracking of learner activity, and automated grading that includes a comprehensive set of instructor resources. eLab can be fully integrated with your LMS, making course management even easier.

▶ *Instructor resources*: This course is also supported on the Labyrinth website with a comprehensive instructor support package that includes detailed lesson plans, PowerPoint presentations, a course syllabus, test banks, additional exercises, and more.

▶ *Learning Resource Center*: The exercise files that accompany this textbook can be found within eLab and on the Learning Resource Center, which may be accessed from the ebook or online at **www.labyrinthelab.com/lrc**.

▶ *Overview chapter content*: The "Overview Chapter ISM" folder in the Instructor Support Materials package and the "Overview Chapter Files" folder in the Student Exercise File download include the helpful "Introducing Microsoft Office and Using Common Features" chapter. In addition to providing a discussion of the various Office versions, this chapter introduces a selection of features common throughout the Office applications. **We recommend that students complete this "overview" chapter first.**

We're excited to share this innovative, new approach with you, and we'd love you to share your experience with us at www.lablearning.com/share.

Display Settings

Multiple factors, including screen resolution, monitor size, and window size, can affect the appearance of the Microsoft Ribbon and its buttons. In this textbook, screen captures were taken at the native (recommended) screen resolutions in Office 2016 running Windows 10, with ClearType enabled.

Visual Conventions

This book uses visual and typographic cues to guide students through the lessons. Some of these cues are described below.

Cue Name	What It Does
`Type this text`	Text you type at the keyboard is printed in this typeface.
Action words	The important action words in exercise steps are presented in boldface.
Ribbon	Glossary terms are highlighted with a light yellow background.
Note! **Tip!** **Warning!**	Tips, notes, and warnings are called out with special icons.
⚠	Videos and WebSims that are a required part of this course are indicated by this icon.
Command→Command→ Command→Command	Commands to execute from the Ribbon are presented like this: Ribbon Tab→Command Group→Command→Subcommand.
☰ **Design→Themes→Themes** 🖼	These notes present shortcut steps for executing certain tasks.

Acknowledgements

Many individuals contribute to the development and completion of a textbook. This book has benefited significantly from the feedback and suggestions of the following reviewers:

Pam Silvers, *Asheville-Buncombe Technical Community College*

Ramiro Villareal, *Brookhaven College*

Teresa Loftis, *Inland Career Education Center*

Kim Pigeon, *Northeast Wisconsin Technical College*

Lynne Kemp, *North Country Community College*

Tom Martin, *Shasta College*

Karen LaPlant, *Hennepin Technical College*

Kay Gerken, *College of DuPage*

Colleen Kennedy, *Spokane Community College*

5 | Using Mail Merge

I n this chapter, you will use the Mail Merge feature to turn boilerplate letters into personalized correspondence. The data source (list of variable information, such as the recipients' addresses) and the main document (form letter) only need to be set up and proofed once. Then you can generate hundreds of letters without checking each one. And you can use Mail Merge for more than letters. You can generate envelopes, labels, legal documents, or just about any fixed-text document that requires variable information. A data source can be a Word document, an Excel worksheet, an Access database, or an Outlook contact list.

LEARNING OBJECTIVES

▸ Build data sources

▸ Create main documents

▸ Perform a mail merge

▸ Deal with merge problems

▸ Generate envelopes and labels

📂 Project: Promoting Exercise Classes

Raritan Clinic East is a pediatric medical practice. The practice serves patients ranging in ages from newborn to eighteen years. As the administrator who oversees the STAYFIT exercise classes at the clinic, once a week you receive the contact information for all new patients who would benefit from these classes. You will send a letter to the patients explaining the program. Once you set up the main document, you will be able to use it over and over for new patients. And once you design a flexible data source, you can use that same source layout for the exercise letters as well as other communications. Mail Merge is a real timesaver.

Introducing Mail Merge

Mail Merge is most often used for generating personalized documents, such as Word letters, mailing labels, and envelopes. But Mail Merge is a versatile tool that can be used with any type of document that combines boilerplate text with variable information, such as email, standard contracts, and legal verbiage. Mail Merge can be a big time-saver and is valuable for managing large mailings.

Components of Mail Merge

Merging creates a document that combines information from two files. They are known as the main document and the data source.

▸ **Main document:** This document controls the merge. It is a Word document that contains the fixed information and merge codes into which the variable information is merged. A typical form letter, for instance, has a different inside address and greeting line in each letter, while the rest of the text is the same for everyone receiving the letter.

▸ **Data source:** The data source can be another Word document, a spreadsheet, a database file, or contact list in Outlook. The data source contains field names that correspond with the merge codes in the main document.

▸ **Merged document:** This document is the result of the merge. It contains all of the letters addressed to each individual in your data source.

You can merge an existing main document with an existing data source, or you can create the main document and data source while stepping through the merge process.

Last Name ▾	First Name ▾	Title ▾	Address Line 1 ▾	City ▾	State ▾	ZIP Code
Adams	Andre	Mr.	2224 Culver Drive	San Diego	CA	92102
Bouras	Talos	Mr.	854 Whitmore Drive	San Diego	CA	92101
Chowdrey	Michael	Mr.	146 Meadow Lane	La Jolla	CA	92103
Navarro	Derek	Mr.	3300 Maple Drive	La Jolla	CA	92103
Romero	Nicole	Ms.	132 Lake Street	San Diego	CA	92102
Wright	Mary	Ms.	1240 Potrero Avenue	San Diego	CA	92101

«AddressBlock»

«GreetingLine»

«First_Name», welcome to Raritan Clinic East, one of the finest clinics in the field of pediatric medicine. As part of our ongoing effort to provide the best patient care, we offer an extensive STAYFIT program. Being active helps you be healthier and stronger—and feel your best. And «Your_Doctor» wants the best for you!

In designing your fitness program, choose from the following offerings:

Aerobic Exercise	Flexibility Training	Strength Training
Dance and Movement	Qi Gong	Calisthenics
Water Aerobics	Tai Chi	Free Weights
Zumba	Yoga	Pilates

Having trouble finding the right exercise program for you? Contact a health coach. Call 1-800-555-0101.

Classes are every evening from 7:00–8:00 p.m. Advanced registration is required. Call 1-800-555-0102.

Sincerely,

Molly Lincoln
STAYFIT Coordinator

The data source can be a Mail Merge recipient list, a Word table, an Excel spreadsheet, or an Access database.

The main document contains standard text and merge codes where variables from the data source will be merged.

Raritan Clinic East

Pediatric Diagnostic Specialists

719 Coronado Drive
San Diego, CA 92102

February 10, 2016

Mr. Andre Adams
2224 Culver Drive
San Diego, CA 92102

Dear Andre:

Andre, welcome to Raritan Clinic East, one of the finest clinics in the field of pediatric medicine. As part of our ongoing effort to provide the best patient care, we offer an extensive STAYFIT program. Being active helps you be healthier and stronger—and feel your best. And Dr. Bey wants the best for you!

In designing your fitness program, choose from the following offerings:

Aerobic Exercise	Flexibility Training	Strength Training
Dance and Movement	Qi Gong	Calisthenics
Water Aerobics	Tai Chi	Free Weights
Zumba	Yoga	Pilates

Having trouble finding the right exercise program for you? Contact a health coach. Call 1-800-555-0101.

Classes are every evening from 7:00–8:00 p.m. Advanced registration is required. Call 1-800-555-0102.

Sincerely,

Molly Lincoln
STAYFIT Coordinator

Here is a completed merge document with the variables from the data source.

The Benefits of Mail Merge

Mail Merge saves a lot of time. Imagine you want to send a letter to 100 customers. Without Mail Merge, you would have to type the same text in all 100 letters (or copy and paste 100 times). However, with Mail Merge, you create one main document with the standard text and one data source containing customer names and addresses.

You will also really appreciate Mail Merge when you later decide you want to make a change. Using Mail Merge, you can edit the main document once and remerge it with the data source to produce a new merged document. Without Mail Merge, you would need to edit each letter individually.

The Mailings Tab

The Mailings tab provides guidance in setting up the main document and data source, and it helps you conduct the merge. The Start Mail Merge group is the beginning point. Alternatively, you can use the Step-by-Step Mail Merge Wizard from the Start Mail Merge menu to walk you through the process.

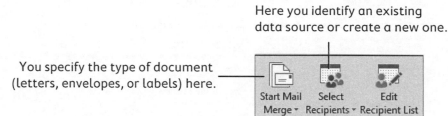

Here you identify an existing data source or create a new one.

You specify the type of document (letters, envelopes, or labels) here.

Working with the Data Source

Data sources typically contain names, addresses, telephone numbers, and other contact information. However, you can include any information in a data source. For example, you could include part numbers and prices to create a parts catalog. You can create a data source in Word, or you can use an external data source, such as an Access database or Excel spreadsheet. Once a data source is created, it can be merged with many different main documents.

 View the video "Designing and Creating a Data Source."

DEVELOP YOUR SKILLS: W5-D1

In this exercise, you will use the Start Mail Merge group on the Ribbon to specify a letter as your main document. Then you will customize the data source columns and enter data.

Before You Begin: *Be sure to visit the Learning Resource Center at labyrinthelab.com/lrc to retrieve the exercise files for this course before beginning this exercise.*

1. Open **W5-D1-ExerciseLtr** from your **Word Chapter 5** folder and save it as **W5-D1-ExerciseLtrRevised**.

2. Choose **Mailings→Start Mail Merge→Start Mail Merge** →**Letters**.

   You are indicating that the letter you just opened will be the main document. Now you will create your mailing list.

3. Choose **Mailings→Start Mail Merge→Select Recipients** 🖼→**Type a New List**.

   The New Address List dialog box opens. Now you will remove unnecessary fields and add a new field.

4. Click **Customize Columns** to open the Customize Address List dialog box.

5. Choose **Company Name** and click **Delete**; click **Yes** to verify the deletion.

6. Delete **Address Line 2**, **Country or Region**, **Home Phone**, **Work Phone**, and **E-mail Address**.

7. Follow these steps to add a field:

Ⓐ Click **Add**.

Ⓑ Type **Your Doctor** and click **OK**.

Ⓒ Click **OK** to close the Customize Address List dialog box.

Enter Records

8. Follow these steps to begin the first record:

   The insertion point should be in the Title field.

Ⓐ Type **Mr.** in the Title field.

Ⓑ Tap Tab to move to the next field.

Tip! *Don't type spaces after entering information in a field; Word will take care of it. You can click a field and make editing changes if necessary.*

9. Type **Talos** and tap Tab to move to the next field.

10. Finish entering the Talos Bouras data shown, tapping Tab between fields. The list of fields will scroll as you Tab and type.

Mr. Talos Bouras	Ms. Nicole Romero	Mr. Michael Chowdrey
854 Whitmore Drive	132 Lake Street	900 C Street
San Diego CA 92101	San Diego CA 92102	La Jolla CA 92103
Dr. Gonzalez	Dr. Mansee	Dr. Kelly

11. When you complete the first record, click **New Entry** or tap Tab to generate a new row for the next record; then enter the two remaining records shown.

Tip! *If you accidentally tap* Tab *after the last record, just click Delete Entry to remove the blank record.*

12. Leave the New Address List dialog box open.

Note! *Always leave your file open at the end of an exercise unless instructed to close it.*

Reviewing Your Records

It's a good idea to review your records for accuracy before saving the data source. However, if you miss an error, you can always edit it later.

New Address List				?	X
Type recipient information in the table. To add more entries, click New Entry.					
Title ▼	First Name ▼	Last Name ▼	Address Line 1	▼ City	▼
▷ Mr.	Talos	Bouras	854 Whitmor	San Diego	

If an entry is wider than the field, position the mouse pointer between column headers and drag to widen (or use the arrow keys to scroll through the entry).

DEVELOP YOUR SKILLS: W5-D2

In this exercise, you will examine your records for accuracy and save your data source.

1. Position the mouse pointer on the scroll bar at the bottom of the dialog box and drag right and left to view all the fields.

2. Follow these steps to review your records:

New Address List				Ⓑ ?	X	
Type recipient information in the table. To add more entries, click New Entry.						
Title ▼	First Name ▼	Last Name ▼	Address Lin... ▼	City	▼	St
▷ Mr.	Talos	Bouras Ⓐ	854 Whitmore D	San Diego		C
Ms.	Nicole	Romero	132 Lake Street	San Diego		C
Mr.	Michael	Chowdrey	900 C Street	La Jolla		C

Ⓐ Position the insertion point here and use the arrow keys to move through the entry.

Ⓑ Position the mouse pointer here and drag to the right to display the entire entry.

3. Review your entry and correct any typos and then click **OK** to open the Save Address List dialog box.

4. Save the data source file as **W5-D2-ExerciseLtrData** in your **Word Chapter 5** folder.

Your data source is now connected to the main document.

Managing the Address List

The Mail Merge Recipients dialog box lets you sort and filter address lists, choose records to include in the mail merge, and edit the data source. If you used a Word table, Excel spreadsheet, or other file for your data source, you can edit directly in that data source file.

⃝! View the video "Working with the Address List."

DEVELOP YOUR SKILLS: W5-D3

In this exercise, you will work with the Mail Merge Recipients dialog box, where you can sort, filter, and edit your mailing list.

1. Choose **Mailings→Start Mail Merge→Select Recipients** 🖾 **→Use an Existing List**.
2. Navigate to your **Word Chapter 5** folder and double-click **W5-D2-ExerciseLtrData**.
3. Choose **Mailings→Start Mail Merge→Edit Recipient List** 🖾.
4. Follow these steps to sort and filter the list and open the Edit Source dialog box:

- **A** Click this field header to sort the list in ascending order by Last Name.
- **B** Click the drop-down arrow and choose **Chowdrey** to filter out other entries. Click the arrow again and choose **(All)** to redisplay all records.
- **C** Click the data source to activate the Edit button.
- **D** Click **Edit** to open the Edit Data Source dialog box.

The Edit Data Source dialog box looks and operates like the New Address List dialog box. The entries appear in the order in which they were originally entered.

5. Follow these steps to edit a record:

- **A** Click this address to select it.
- **B** Type **146 Meadow Lane** in its place.

6. Follow these guidelines to enter the three records in the following illustration:
   - Click the **New Entry** button or tap Tab at the end of the row for each new record.
   - Tap Tab to move from one field to the next.
   - If you accidentally tap Tab after the last record, use Delete Entry to remove the blank record.

Ms. Mary Wright	Mr. Derek Navarro	Mr. Andre Adams
1240 Potrero Avenue	3300 Maple Drive	2224 Culver Drive
San Diego CA 92101	La Jolla CA 92103	San Diego CA 92102
Dr. Gonzalez	Dr. Storm	Dr. Bey

7. Review the entries for accuracy and then click **OK** to close the dialog box.

8. Click **Yes** when the message appears verifying your update.

9. Click **OK** to close the Mail Merge Recipients dialog box.

Working with the Main Document

You accomplish a merge by combining a main document with a data source. Merge fields in a main document correspond to fields in the data source. Some merge codes, such as the Address Block code, are composite codes consisting of a number of grouped fields. For example, the Address Block code includes Title, First Name, Last Name, Address, City, State, and Zip.

 View the video "Inserting Merge Fields in the Main Document."

DEVELOP YOUR SKILLS: W5-D4

In this exercise, you will set up a form letter. The exercise letter main document should still be open.

1. If necessary, choose **Home→Paragraph→Show/Hide** ¶ to display formatting characters.

2. Select the **Today's Date** line and tap Delete.

3. Choose **Insert→Text→Date & Time** 📅.

4. Choose the third date format, check **Update Automatically**, and click **OK**.

   Checking the Update Automatically option means the date in your letter will always be the current date, which is a convenient option for form letters that you want to use again.

5. Tap Enter four times after inserting the date.

   Now you will insert the Address Block code.

6. Choose **Mailings→Write & Insert Fields→Address Block** 📄.

   The Insert Address Block dialog box allows you to choose a format for the address block.

7. Follow these steps to insert an Address Block code:

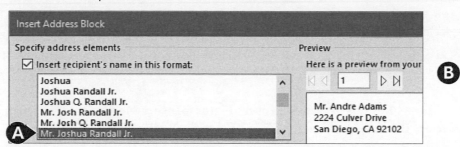

Ⓐ Choose different formats and view the preview on the right; then choose **Mr. Joshua Randall Jr.**

Ⓑ Leave the remaining options as shown and click **OK**.

The <<AddressBlock>> code appears in the letter. During the merge, the information from the data source will be inserted at the Address Block code location.

8. Tap [Enter] twice.

Now you will insert the Greeting Line code.

9. Choose **Mailings→Write & Insert Fields→Greeting Line** 📄.

10. Follow these steps to modify and insert the Greeting Line code:

Ⓐ Change this option to a **colon (:)**.

Ⓑ Note the generic greeting that will be used for data records if they are missing last names.

Ⓒ Choose **Joshua** from the list and then click **OK**.

11. Tap [Enter] twice.

12. Follow these steps to insert the First Name code into the letter:

Ⓐ If necessary, position the insertion point to the left of *Welcome*.

Ⓑ Click the **Insert Merge Field menu** button ▾.

Ⓒ Choose **First_Name**.

13. Type a comma and tap [Spacebar], then delete the uppercase *W* and replace it with a lowercase *w*.

14. Position the insertion point to the left of *wants* as shown.

«First_Name», welcome to Raritan Clinic East, one of the finest clinics in the field of pediatric medicine. As part of our ongoing effort to provide the best patient care, we offer an extensive STAYFIT program. Being active helps you be healthier and stronger—and feel your best. And wants the best for you!¶

15. Choose **Mailings→Write & Insert Fields→Insert Merge Field** 📇 **menu button** ▾, choose **Your_Doctor**, and then tap [Spacebar].

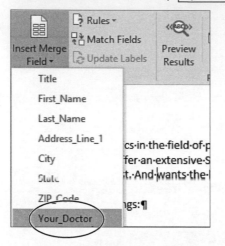

16. Take time to review your letter, making sure the merge fields match this example. In particular, make sure you use the proper punctuation between fields and the text.

The merge fields are highlighted in this figure to help you locate them; your merge fields do not need to be highlighted. (The Highlight Merge Fields button is in the Write & Insert Fields group.)

«AddressBlock»

«GreetingLine»

«First_Name», welcome to Raritan Clinic East, one of the finest clinics in the field of pediatric medicine. As part of our ongoing effort to provide the best patient care, we offer an extensive STAYFIT program. Being active helps you be healthier and stronger—and feel your best. And «Your_Doctor» wants the best for you!

 Any punctuation or spacing errors that occur in your main document will appear in every merged letter.

17. Choose **Home→Paragraph→Show/Hide** ¶ to turn off formatting marks.

18. Save your file.

Conducting a Merge

Merging combines a main document with a data source document. If you are merging a form letter with a data source, Word produces a personalized copy of the form letter for each record in the data source.

It's always a good idea to preview the merge results before you complete the merge so you can make any corrections. If you notice an error that needs to be fixed in the main document, simply click Preview Results again to return to the main document.

Use this button to display the first record from your data source in the letter. ⎯ Preview Results

Navigate through the letters with these buttons.

Find Recipient

Check for Errors ⎯ You can click here to have Word check for errors, such as an invalid field code.

Preview Results

When you feel confident that your letter and data source are accurate, you are ready to complete the merge.

Finish & Merge ▾

This option merges letters on the screen so you can edit individual letters, if desired. ⎯ Edit Individual Documents...

Print Documents... ⎯ This choice merges directly to the printer.

Send Email Messages...

You can also merge to email messages.

To Save or Not to Save?

Merged documents are rarely saved because they can easily be reconstructed by merging the main document with the data source. Instead, merged documents are usually previewed, printed, and closed without saving. But you can certainly save the merged document if you wish to have a record of it. If a merged document contains errors, you can close it without saving, edit the main document or data source, and conduct the merge again.

DEVELOP YOUR SKILLS: W5-D5

In this exercise, you will use the Preview Results command to review your letters then you will complete the merge on the screen.

1. If necessary, switch to the **Mailings** tab.

2. Follow these steps to preview the merge:

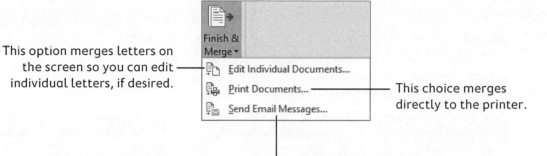

Address Block   Greeting Line   Insert Merge Field ▾   Rules ▾   Match Fields   Update Labels   Preview Results   Find Recipient   Check for Errors

Write & Insert Fields

Preview Results

Mr. Andre Adams
2224 Culver Drive
San Diego, CA 92102

Ⓐ Click **Preview Results** to display the first inside address.

Ⓑ Use the navigation buttons to scroll through all of your merged documents.

3. Choose **Mailings→Finish→Finish & Merge** 📄→**Edit Individual Documents**.

4. Click **OK** to merge all records.

5. Scroll through the letters and scan their contents.

   Notice that there is one letter for each record in the data source.

6. Close the merged document without saving.

7. Choose **Mailings→Preview Results→Preview Results** 🔍 again to display the main document instead of the previews.

Working with Merge Problems

Several common errors can cause a merge to produce incorrect results. The merged document (or preview) will usually provide clues as to why a merge fails to produce the intended results. Once you identify an error in the merged document, such as leaving out a comma or space before or after a merge field, you can then conduct the merge again to determine if the error was fixed. Repeat this process until the merge works as intended.

COMMON MERGE PROBLEMS

Problem	Solution
The same error appears in every merge letter.	The problem is in the main document. Correct the error and perform the merge again.
Some letters are missing data.	Some records in the data source are missing data. Add data and perform the merge again.
Some letters have incorrect data.	Some records in the data source are incorrect. Correct the errors and perform the merge again.

DEVELOP YOUR SKILLS: W5-D6

In this exercise, you will examine your document for merge problems. This exercise does not address all possible merge problems; it does, however, address one specific error that you will make intentionally. You will insert a colon after the Greeting Line code.

1. Position the insertion point after <<GreetingLine>> and type a colon.

2. Choose **Mailings→Finish→Finish & Merge** 📄→**Edit Individual Documents**.

3. Click **OK** to merge all records.

4. Browse through the merged document and notice there are two colons following the greeting line in every letter.

   Because the error occurs in every letter, you know the error is in the main document.

5. Locate any other errors and notice how often the errors occur (in every merged letter or just one).

   Next you will correct the double colon error and any other errors you discovered that occurred in all letters.

6. Close the merged document without saving; then remove the colon following <<GreetingLine>> and save the main document.

7. Follow these guidelines if you find a data error in just one letter.
   - Choose **Mailings→Start Mail Merge→Edit Recipient List** 📇.
   - In the Mail Merge Recipients dialog box, highlight the data source in the bottom-left corner and click **Edit**.
   - Fix any errors and click **OK**; click **Yes** to update the data.
   - Click **OK** to close the dialog box.
8. When you have corrected any errors, execute the merge again.
9. Close the merged document without saving it and then save and close the exercise letter main document.

Merging Envelopes and Labels

When you begin a mail merge, you are presented with options for the type of main document you can create. In addition to form letters, you can choose envelopes, labels, and other types of documents. You can use the same data source for various main documents. For example, you can use the same data source for envelopes and mailing labels that you used for the form letter.

Generating Envelopes with Mail Merge

Mail Merge lets you choose the envelope size and formats. The standard business (Size 10) envelope is the default. Check your printer manual for instructions on loading envelopes.

Various envelope sizes are available.

Here you can choose the font and positions of the delivery and return addresses.

DEVELOP YOUR SKILLS: W5-D7

In this exercise, you will choose an envelope as the main document and connect the exercise letter data file to the envelope.

1. Start a new, blank document.
2. Choose **Mailings→Start Mail Merge→Start Mail Merge** 📄**→Envelopes**.
3. In the Envelope Options dialog box, if necessary, choose **Size 10** as the envelope size and click **OK**.
   Now you will attach the same data source that you used for your letter.
4. Choose **Mailings→Start Mail Merge→Select Recipients** 📇**→Use an Existing List**.
5. In the Select Data Source dialog box, navigate to your **Word Chapter 5** folder and open **W5-D2-ExerciseLtrData**.

Arranging the Envelope

You can insert an Address Block code in the envelope main document just as you do for form letter main documents. If you are not using envelopes with preprinted return addresses, you can type your return address. You save an envelope main document like any other main document.

DEVELOP YOUR SKILLS: W5-D8

In this exercise, you will place the return address and the Address Block code on the envelope. Then you will merge the envelope main document with the data source.

1. If necessary, display formatting marks.
2. Type this return address, starting at the first paragraph symbol in the upper-left corner of the envelope:

   Raritan Clinic East
   719 Coronado Drive
   San Diego, CA   92102

3. Position the insertion point next to the paragraph symbol toward the center of the envelope.
4. Choose **Mailings→Write & Insert Fields→Address Block** 📄.
5. Click **OK** to accept the default address block settings.

   The address information from the data source will appear in this location. Now you will preview the merge.

6. Choose **Mailings→Preview Results→Preview Results** 🔍 to display a record from the data source in the envelope.
7. Use the navigation buttons in the Preview Results group to scroll through all of your merged envelopes.
8. Choose **Mailings→Finish→Finish & Merge** 📄→**Edit Individual Documents** and click **OK** to merge all records.
9. Turn off formatting marks and then scroll through the envelopes and notice that there is one envelope for each record in the data source.

   You could use the envelopes for mailing the letters created in the previous exercises. Each letter would have a corresponding envelope because they are generated from the same data source.

10. If necessary, fix any problems with the mail merge and merge the envelopes again.
11. Close the merged document without saving it.
12. Choose **Mailings→Preview Results→Preview Results** 🔍 to turn off the preview.
13. Save the main document envelope as **W5-D8-ExerciseLtrEnv** in your **Word Chapter 5** folder and then close it.

Generating Labels with Mail Merge

You can use Mail Merge to generate mailing labels for each record in a data source. Mail Merge lets you choose the label format, sheet size, and other specifications. It also lets you insert an Address Block code and other codes in the main document. Like other main documents, a label main document can be saved for future use.

 View the video "Using Label Options."

DEVELOP YOUR SKILLS: W5-D9

In this exercise, you will set up a labels main document and merge it with the data source used in the previous exercises.

1. Start a new, blank document and, if necessary, display formatting marks.
2. Choose **Mailings→Start Mail Merge→Start Mail Merge** 📄**→Labels**.
3. Follow these steps to choose a printer option and a label:

Ⓐ Choose **Default Tray**. The text in parentheses may vary based on the printer model.

Ⓑ Choose **Avery US Letter**.

Ⓒ Choose **5160 Easy Peel Address Labels** and click **OK**.

The labels main document appears in the window. Labels are contained in a Word table, but don't worry. You don't have to be a table expert to create labels.

Connect the Data Source

4. Choose **Mailings→Start Mail Merge→Select Recipients** 🗃**→Use an Existing List**.
5. In the Select Data Source dialog box, navigate to your **Word Chapter 5** folder and open **W5-D2-ExerciseLtrData**.
6. Make sure the insertion point is next to the paragraph symbol in the first address label.

   Notice that the space for the first label is blank and all the rest have a Next Record code in them. Now you will add the Address Block code.

7. Choose **Mailings→Write & Insert Fields→Address Block** 📄 and click **OK**.
8. Choose **Mailings→Write & Insert Fields→Update Labels** 🗒 to place the Address Block code in all labels.

   Your address will fit the labels better if you remove the additional spacing.

9. Select the table and choose **Layout→Paragraph**; then type **0** in the **Before** field and tap Enter.
10. Choose **Mailings→Preview Results→Preview Results** 🔍 to see how the labels will look when you print them.
11. Turn off Preview Results when you are finished.

Conduct the Merge

12. Choose **Mailings→Finish→Finish & Merge** **→Edit Individual Documents**.

13. Click **OK** to merge all the records.

14. Close your merged document without saving it.

15. Save the labels main document in your **Word Chapter 5** folder as `W5-D9-MergeLabels`.

16. Close the document and then exit Word.

Self-Assessment

Check your knowledge of this chapter's key concepts and skills using the Self-Assessment in your ebook or eLab course.

Reinforce Your Skills

Create a Data Source and Main Document

In this exercise, you will create a data source and main document for a Kids for Change mailing. The kids are holding a fund-raiser for a microlending project that focuses on providing economic opportunities for entrepreneurs in India. They will conduct a mailing to announce the upcoming project and canvass their neighborhoods for donations.

1. Start Word, open **W5-R1-Fundraiser** from your **Word Chapter 5** folder, and save it as **W5-R1-FundraiserRevised**.
2. Choose **Mailings→Start Mail Merge→Start Mail Merge** 📄 **→Letters** to identify the fund-raising letter as the main document.
3. Choose **Mailings→Start Mail Merge→Select Recipients→Type a New List**.
4. Click **Customize Columns**.
5. Click **Address Line 2** and click **Delete**; click **Yes** to confirm the deletion.
6. Also delete the following fields:
   - Country or Region
   - Home Phone
   - Work Phone
   - E-mail Address
7. Click **Add**, type **Member First Name**, and then click **OK**.
8. Also add a field called **Member Last Name** and then click **OK** twice.
9. With the insertion point in the **Title** field, type **Ms.** and tap Tab.
10. Follow these guidelines to complete the data source list:
    - Continue typing and tabbing to complete the first record shown.
    - Be sure to include the member first name, Eric, and last name, Speck, in the first record.
    - Tap Tab to begin a new record and then continue typing and tabbing to enter the next three records.
    - Note that there is no company information for the third record; Tab through that field.
    - If you accidentally tap Tab following the last record, use the **Delete Entry** button to remove the blank record.

Ms. Loretta Morales Morales Super Market 311 Ocean Street Miami FL 33130	Mr. Tony D'Agusto Tony's Trattoria 675 Miller Ave. Miami FL 33129	Mr. Allan Morgan 951 4th Street Miami FL 33136	Ms. Margarita Elizondo Elan Fashions 307 Dolphin Way Miami FL 33136
Member: Eric Speck	**Member:** Wendy Chang	**Member:** Stella Hopkins	**Member:** Diego Cantero

11. Review your records for accuracy; click **OK** when you are satisfied with your work.
12. Save the data source in your **Word Chapter 5** folder as **W5-R1-FundraiserData**.

Set Up the Main Document

13. In the fundraiser letter, select **[Inside Address]** (but not the paragraph symbol at the end of the line) and tap `Delete`.

14. Choose **Mailings→Write & Insert Fields→Address Block** 🖹 and then click **OK** to accept the default address block settings.

15. Delete **[Name]** in the greeting line but not the paragraph symbol at the end of the line.

16. Choose **Mailings→Write & Insert Fields→Greeting Line**.

17. Choose **Joshua** and **colon** in the Greeting Line Format area as shown and click **OK**.

18. In the last sentence of the first paragraph, delete **[Member Name]**.

19. Choose **Mailings→Write & Insert Fields→Insert Merge Field menu button** ▼→ **Member_First_Name**.

20. Tap `Spacebar` and insert the **Member_Last_Name** field.

21. Save and close the letter.

REINFORCE YOUR SKILLS: W5-R2

Merge a Letter, Envelopes, and Labels

Kids for Change is starting an after-school tutoring program. The tutoring supervisor will send form letters to parents announcing the program. In this exercise, you will merge a data source with a letter. You will also merge the data source with envelopes and labels.

1. Open **W5-R2-ParentLtr** from your **Word Chapter 5** folder and save it as **W5-R2-ParentLtrRevised**.

Notice the merge fields in the letter, including four merge fields in the body of the letter, and that <<Child_Name>> appears twice.

2. Choose **Mailings→Start Mail Merge→Start Mail Merge** 🖹→**Letters**.

3. Choose **Mailings→Start Mail Merge→Select Recipients→Use an Existing List**.

4. Navigate to your **Word Chapter 5** folder and open **W5-R2-ParentData**.

5. Choose **Mailings→Preview Results→Preview Results**.

6. Scroll through the letters and then turn off **Preview Results**.

7. Choose **Mailings→Finish→Finish & Merge** 🖹→**Edit Individual Documents** and then click **OK** to merge all records.

8. Scroll through the merged letters; close the file without saving it.

9. Save and close the parent letter main document.

Generate Envelopes

10. Start a new, blank document.

11. Choose **Mailings→Start Mail Merge→Start Mail Merge→Envelopes**.

12. Click **OK** to accept the envelope defaults.

13. Choose **Mailings→Start Mail Merge→Select Recipients→Use an Existing List**.

14. Navigate to your **Word Chapter 5** folder and open **W5-R2-ParentData** to attach the data source to the envelope.

15. If necessary, display formatting marks; then type this return address at the first paragraph symbol in the upper-left corner of the envelope:

```
Kids for Change
726 Throckmorton Ave.
Sacramento, CA   95613
```

16. Position the insertion point next to the paragraph symbol toward the center of the envelope.

17. Choose **Mailings→Write & Insert Fields→Address Block**; click **OK** to accept the address block defaults.

18. Choose **Mailings→Preview Results→Preview Results**.

19. Navigate through the records and then turn off **Preview Results**.

20. Save the envelope as **W5-R2-ParentEnv**; close the envelope file.

Generate Mailing Labels

21. Start a new, blank document.

22. Choose **Mailings→Start Mail Merge→Start Mail Merge→Labels**.

23. If necessary, choose **Avery US Letter** as the Label Vendor and **5160 Easy Peel Address Labels** as the Product Number and then click **OK**.

24. Choose **Mailings→Start Mail Merge→Select Recipients→Use an Existing List**.

25. Navigate to your **Word Chapter 5** folder and open **W5-R2-Parent Data**.

26. Display formatting marks, if necessary, and then make sure the insertion point is next to the paragraph symbol in the first label.

27. Choose **Mailings→Write & Insert Fields→Address Block**; click **OK** to accept the address block defaults.

28. Choose **Mailings→Write & Insert Fields→Update Labels** ⧉ to insert the Address Block code on all labels.

29. Choose **Mailings→Preview Results→Preview Results** to verify all labels will print correctly.

Because the addresses are three lines, they fit on the Avery 5160 labels without removing extra spacing.

30. Turn off **Preview Results** to return to the labels main document.

31. Save the labels file as **W5-R2-ParentLabels** in your **Word Chapter 5** folder.

32. Close the file.

Merge Letters and Envelopes

Kids for Change is sponsoring a walkathon fund-raiser to buy musical instruments for the local elementary school. The walkathon supervisor will be contacting Kids for Change members and encouraging their participation. In this exercise, you will designate a letter as the main document and create a data source. Then you will preview the results and correct any merge problems before conducting the merge. Finally, you will generate envelopes for the letters.

1. Open **W5-R3-Walkers** from your **Word Lesson 5** folder and save it as **W5-R3-WalkersRevised**.

2. Choose **Mailings→Start Mail Merge→Start Mail Merge→Letters** to designate the Walkers letter as the main document.

3. Choose **Mailings→Start Mail Merge→Select Recipients→Type a New List**.

   Now you will customize the data source columns.

4. Click **Customize Columns** to display the Customize Address List dialog box.

5. Click **Company Name** and click **Delete**; click **Yes** to confirm the deletion.

6. Delete the following fields and then click **OK**:
   - Address Line 2
   - Country or Region
   - Work Phone
   - E-mail Address

7. Place the insertion point in the **Title** field, type **Mr.**, and tap ⎄Tab to move to the next field.

8. Type **Sean** in the **First Name** field, tap ⎄Tab, and type **Corn** in the **Last Name** field.

9. Continue tabbing and typing to complete the Sean Corn record as shown, tap ⎄Tab to begin the next record, and then enter the remaining records.

Mr. Sean Corn 308 Alhambra Avenue Monterey CA 93940 831-555-0134	Mr. Craig Dostie 31200 Erwin Street Monterey CA 93940 831-555-0167	Ms. Alexia Lopez 2134 Harbor Blvd. Monterey CA 93942 831-555-0132
Ms. Margaret Wong 1308 West Ramona Blvd. Monterey CA 93940 831-555-0198	Ms. Phyllis Coen 4745 Buffin Avenue Monterey CA 93943 831-555-0178	Mr. Winston Boey 263 East Howard Street Monterey CA 93944 831-555-0196

10. Review your records for accuracy and make any necessary corrections.

    Now you will sort your list by Last Name.

11. Click the **Last Name** column header to sort the list alphabetically in ascending order and then click **OK**.

12. Navigate to your **Word Chapter 5** folder and save the file as **W5-R3-WalkersData**.

Set Up the Main Document and Correct Merge Problems

13. Follow these guidelines to insert the merge codes:

- Replace *INSIDE ADRESS* with the **Address Block** code using the default formats.
- Replace *GREETING LINE* with the **Greeting Line** code, changing the Greeting Line Format name to **Joshua**.
- In the last paragraph, replace *HOME PHONE* with the **Home_Phone** code.

14. Use the **Preview Results** feature to review your letters, correct any errors in the main document, and then turn off Preview Results.

Phyllis Cohen's name is misspelled in the data source. You will make that correction now.

15. Choose **Mailings→Start Mail Merge→Edit Recipient List** 📝.

16. Click the data source in the bottom-left corner and click **Edit**.

17. Change the spelling from *Coen* to **Cohen** and then click **OK**.

18. Click **Yes** to verify the update and then click **OK** to close the Mail Merge Recipients dialog box.

19. Use the navigation buttons in the Preview Results group to verify the change to the data source and any changes you made to the main document, and then turn off **Preview Results**.

20. Choose **Mailings→Finish→Finish & Merge** 📄→**Edit Individual Documents** and then click **OK**.

21. Scroll through your letters and then close the merged document without saving it; save and close the main document letter.

Merge Envelopes

22. Start a new, blank document.

23. Choose **Mailings→Start Mail Merge→Start Mail Merge→Envelopes**.

24. Make sure the envelope is **Size 10** and click **OK**.

Now you will attach the data source to your envelope.

25. Choose **Mailings→Start Mail Merge→Select Recipients** 📇→**Use an Existing List**.

26. Navigate to your **Word Chapter 5** folder and open **W5-R3-WalkersData**.

27. If necessary, turn on formatting marks; then type this return address at the top paragraph symbol in the upper-left corner of the envelope:

```
Kids for Change
456 Bayside Road
Monterey, CA  93943
```

28. Position the insertion point next to the paragraph symbol toward the middle of the envelope.

29. Choose **Mailings→Write & Insert Fields→Address Block** and then click **OK**.

30. Choose **Mailings→Preview Results→Preview Results**.

31. Use the navigation buttons to view all envelopes and then turn off the preview.

32. Choose **Mailings→Finish→Finish & Merge→Edit Individual Documents** and then click **OK**.

33. Scroll through the envelopes and then close the file without saving it.

34. Save the envelope main document as **W5-R3-WalkersEnv** in your **Word Chapter 5** folder; close the document.

✏ Apply Your Skills

Create a Data Source and Main Document

Universal Corporate Events is announcing a new affordable and flexible program for its small-business clients. In this exercise, you will create a small-business client data source, and you will review the records and sort the list. Then you will specify a letter as a main document and insert merge fields in the letter.

1. Open **W5-A1-SmallBiz** from your **Word Chapter 5** folder and save it as **W5-A1-SmallBizRevised**.

2. Specify the Small Biz letter as the main document.

   Now you will customize the columns for your new data source.

3. Delete and add columns as needed to create the following fields in your data source:

   - Title
   - First Name
   - Last Name
   - Company Name
   - Address Line 1
   - City
   - State
   - Zip Code
   - Agent Name

4. Add these records to your data source:

Mr. Tony Simpson	Mr. Jason Jones	Ms. Debbie Thomas
Bigger Time Video Distributors	Move It Distribution	Barker Books
312 York Lane	2233 Crystal Street	497 Tennessee Street
Richmond CA 94804	San Mateo CA 94403	Richmond CA 94804
Agent Name: David Roth	**Agent Name:** Tammy Nelson	**Agent Name:** Jacob Williams

5. Sort the data source in ascending alphabetic order by **Company Name**.

6. Save the data source as **W5-A1-SmallBizData** in your **Word Chapter 5** folder.

7. Delete the *Today's Date* placeholder, choose **Insert→Text→Date & Time** 📅, choose the third date format, and make sure **Update Automatically** is checked.

8. Follow these guidelines for inserting merge codes in the main document:

   - Replace *INSIDE ADDRESS* with the **Address Block** code using the default formats.
   - Replace *GREETING LINE* with the **Greeting Line** code and change the ending punctuation to a colon.
   - In the last paragraph, replace *AGENT NAME* with the **Agent_Name** code.

9. Preview the letters and check that the spacing is correct and then turn off the preview and make any needed changes.

10. Save and close the letter.

APPLY YOUR SKILLS: W5-A2

Complete a Merge

Universal Corporate Events is conducting a seminar on visa requirements for United States citizens. It is sending a form letter invitation to its clients' in-house travel agents. In this exercise, you will merge letters, envelopes, and labels. You will also correct merge problems.

1. Open **W5-A2-VisaLtr** from your **Word Chapter 5** folder and save it as **W5-A2-VisaLtrRevised**.

2. Designate the letter as the main document and **W5-A2-VisaData** from your **Word Chapter 5** folder as the data source.

3. Preview the merge and notice that there is an error in the greeting line.

4. Close the preview and then edit the main document and preview the letters again, checking that the greeting line is correct.

5. Close the preview; save and close the main document.

Merge Envelopes and Labels

6. Start a new, blank document and create a **Size 10** envelope as the main document with this return address:
   Suzanne Frost, Sales Manager
   Universal Corporate Events
   129 Potter Road
   Middlefield, CT   06455

7. Attach **W5-A2-VisaData** as the data source for the envelopes.

8. Insert an **Address Block** code in the middle of the envelope using the default formats.

9. Preview the envelopes.

10. Save the envelope main document in your **Word Chapter 5** folder as **W5-A2-VisaEnv** and then close it.

11. Start a new, blank document and create a label main document using **Avery US Letter** as the Label Vendor and **5160 Easy Peel Address Labels** as the Product Number.

12. Attach **W5-A2-VisaData** as the data source.

13. Insert the **Address Block** code in the first label using the default formats and use the **Update Labels** command to replicate the Address Block code on all labels.

14. Preview the results and notice that the addresses don't fit well on the labels.

15. Close the preview, select the labels table, and remove Word's extra spacing by entering **0** in the **Before** field.

    Hint: The Before field is at Layout→Paragraph.

16. Preview the results again to ensure that the labels fit correctly.

17. Close the preview and save the labels main document in your **Word Chapter 5** folder as **W5-A2-VisaLabels**.

18. Close the labels main document.

Create a Mail Merge for Trip Winners

A Universal Corporate Events client is rewarding its top sales performers with a trip to Tokyo. It will send an itinerary letter to the company's winners. In this exercise, you will create a data source using customized columns and add merge codes to main documents. You will preview and merge the main documents with the data source, make an editing change to a record, and sort the data source.

1. Open **W5-A3-TokyoLtr** from your **Word Chapter 5** folder and save it as **W5-A3-TokyoLtrRevised**.

2. Specify the letter as the main document and then start a new data source list.

3. Customize the columns by deleting some fields and keeping the fields shown here:
   - Title
   - First Name
   - Last Name
   - Company Name
   - Address Line 1
   - City
   - State
   - Zip Code

4. Create the data source using these three records and save it as **W5-A3-TokyoData**.

Ms. Jasleen Mahal	Mr. George Iverson	Mr. Anthony Waldek
Superior Storage Devices	Superior Storage Devices	Superior Storage Devices
951 Industrial Way	951 Industrial Way	951 Industrial Way
Trenton NJ 08601	Trenton NJ 08601	Trenton NJ 08601

5. Follow these guidelines to insert merge codes in the letter:
   - Replace *INSIDE ADDRESS* with **Address Block** code using the default formats.
   - Replace *GREETING LINE* with **Greeting Line** code using the default formats.
   - In the first paragraph, replace *COMPANY NAME* with the **Company_Name** code.
   - In the last paragraph, replace *FIRST NAME* with the **First_Name** code.

Preview the Merge Results

6. Preview the merge, make sure the spacing is correct, and then close the preview.

7. Modify the spacing in the main document if necessary.

   You want the greeting line to be less formal, so you will change the format to the recipient's first name.

8. Right-click the **Greeting Line** code and choose **Edit Greeting Line** from the menu.

9. In the Greeting Line Format area, click the drop-down arrow next to Mr. Randall, choose **Joshua** from the list, and click **OK**.

10. Preview the letters again to ensure the change was made and then turn off the preview.

11. Merge the letter with the data source, choosing **Edit Individual Documents**, and then scroll through the letters.

12. Close the merged document without saving it; save and close the main document.

Merge Envelopes and Labels

13. Start a new, blank document, designate it as a mail merge envelope, and use a **Size 10** envelope.

14. Insert this return address on the envelope:

```
Ms. Tasha Reynolds
Universal Corporate Events
456 Riverview Road
Trenton, NJ   08601
```

15. Attach the Tokyo data source to the envelope and insert the **Address Block** code using defaults.

16. Merge the envelopes and check them for accuracy; if necessary, correct any errors and conduct the merge again.

17. Close the merge document without saving it.

18. Save the envelope main document as **W5-A3-TokyoEnv** and then close it.

19. Start a new, blank document and designate it as **Labels**.

20. Choose **Avery US Letter** as the Label Vendor and **5160** as the Product Number.

21. Attach the Tokyo data source, insert the **Address Block** code in the first label, and update the labels to replicate the **Address Block** code in all labels.

22. Preview the labels and notice the addresses don't fit well because of Word's extra spacing.

23. Close the preview, select the labels table, and remove the extra spacing.

24. Preview the labels again to verify the change in spacing and then close the preview.

25. Save the labels main document as **W5-A3-TokyoLabels** and then close it.

◢ Extend Your Skills

These exercises challenge you to think critically and apply your new skills. You will be evaluated on your ability to follow directions, completeness, creativity, and the use of proper grammar and mechanics. Save files to your chapter folder. Submit assignments as directed.

W5-E1 That's the Way I See It

You are planning a field trip for the fifth grade class you teach. Create a permission letter informing parents of the trip and how it relates to students' school work (e.g., visiting an aquarium after studying about ocean life). Include a request for parents to sign and return the letter. Save the letter as **W5-E1-FieldTripLtr**.

Create a three-record data source of parent names and addresses and any other variables you choose. Customize the data source with only the column headings you need. Save the data source as **W5-E1-FieldTripData**. Insert merge codes in the form letter and merge the main document and data source. Save the merged document as **W5-E1-FieldTripLtrMerged**. Create an envelope main document with your return address, merge it with your data file, and save it as **W5-E1-FieldTripEnvMerged**.

W5-E2 Be Your Own Boss

You are introducing a rewards program for Blue Jean Landscaping customers. Create a form letter of two to three paragraphs describing how customers can accumulate points toward purchases. Mention three other benefits (make them up) for program members. Save the letter as **W5-E2-RewardsLtr**.

Create a data source of three customers' names and addresses and any other fields you want to use. Customize the data source for only those columns needed and save it as **W5-E2-RewardsData**. Insert merge field codes in the letter and conduct the merge, saving the merged document as **W5-E2-RewardsLtrMerged**. Finally, create a labels document named **W5-E2-RewardsLabels** and merge it with the data source. Save the merged labels as **W5-E2-RewardsLabelsMerged**.

W5-E3 Demonstrate Proficiency

Stormy BBQ has added brisket of beef to its menu! They offered a free beef brisket meal and a $20 gift certificate to the first five customers who visited their restaurant on New Year's Day. They plan to mail the certificates to the qualifying customers. As a Stormy BBQ employee, you have been asked to compose a congratulatory letter to go with the certificates.

Compose an appropriate letter of two or three paragraphs saved as **W5-E3-CertLtr**. Create a name and address data source for five winners. Customize the data source by adding any fields you want to use in your letter; delete any fields you don't intend to use. Save the data source as **W5-E3-CertData**. Merge the letter and the data source and save the merge document as **W5-E3-CertLtrMerged**. Finally, create an envelope main document to go with the mailing and include Stormy BBQ's return address and the Address Block code on a Size 10 envelope. Save the envelope main document as **W5-E3-CertEnv**. Preview the envelopes to verify that they will print correctly. Make corrections if necessary, merge the envelope with your data source, and then save the merged document as **W5-E3-CertEnvMerged**.

WORD

6 | Creating a Newsletter

A newsletter should be an essential part of every organization's communication plan. It's a great way to rally support for new programs or products and to maintain an ongoing relationship with your clients. In this chapter, you will create engaging newsletters using graphics and special text effects to add eye appeal. Finally, you will add a cover page to give a professional touch to your newsletter.

LEARNING OBJECTIVES

▸ Add graphic effects

▸ Use section breaks and columns

▸ Wrap text around a graphic image

▸ Insert a cover page

▸ Print part of a full document

📁 Project: Creating a Client Newsletter

As a leading pediatric facility, Raritan Clinic East stays ahead of the curve by updating its protocols with the latest discoveries. It stays in regular contact with its patient population through a monthly newsletter. As an administrator for the clinic, you have been asked to publish this month's newsletter, which describes meningitis, its symptoms, where outbreaks are likely to occur, and its treatment. You will add interest to your newsletter by using graphics and special text formatting.

📖 Six Tips for an Effective Newsletter

A newsletter is an effective way to keep in touch with clients. It adds a personal touch that can create a bond between your organization and the reader.

- ▶ Know your audience.
- ▶ Have a compelling opening line.
- ▶ Use a clean, simple layout with plenty of white space.
- ▶ Be informative and educational and provide true value.
- ▶ Use graphics but don't overdo it.
- ▶ Insert headings and subheadings to chunk your information into easy-to-read segments.

Adding Special Effects to Text

To add interest and dimension to newsletters, you can use graphic effects. For example, you can add WordArt for flair. You can create WordArt by adding your own text to a WordArt object, or you can apply a WordArt object to existing text. Either way, you have a full array of WordArt formatting tools available on the contextual Drawing Tools Format tab.

Font effects are interesting, special treatments of text. Options include strikethrough, superscript/subscript, small caps, and all caps.

☰ Insert→Text→WordArt 𝒜

☰ Home→Font→dialog box launcher ⌐

DEVELOP YOUR SKILLS: W6-D1

In this exercise, you will begin creating the newsletter for Raritan Clinic East. You will start with a WordArt heading, which you will format with a new fill color, font color, and text effects. Then you will use the Font dialog box to adjust the font style and size, and then you will add font effects.

1. Start Word; open a new, blank document; and save it to your **Word Chapter 6** folder as **W6-D1-RaritanNewsltr**.

2. Display formatting marks and then type these heading lines at the top of the document:

   Raritan Clinic East
   The Children's Clinic
   November, 2016

3. Tap ⌷Enter⌷ three times.

4. Select *Raritan Clinic East* but do not select the paragraph mark at the end of the line.

5. Choose **Insert→Text→WordArt** 4 and then choose **Fill – Blue, Accent 1, Shadow**.

6. With the WordArt object selected, follow these steps to place it in line with the text:

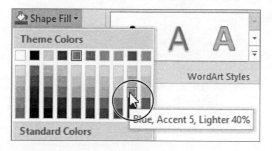

   Ⓐ Click the **Layout Options** smart tag.

   Ⓑ Choose **In Line with Text** and then click in the document to close the gallery.

7. Click the border of the WordArt to select the entire object.

8. Choose **Drawing Tools→Format→Shape Styles→Shape Fill menu button** ▾ and then choose **Blue, Accent 5, Lighter 40%** from the gallery.

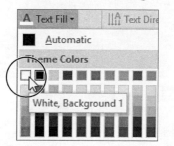

9. Choose **Drawing Tools→Format→WordArt Styles→Text Fill menu button** ▾ and then choose **White, Background 1**.

10. With the object selected, choose **Drawing Tools→Format→WordArt Styles→Text Effects** Ⓐ.

11. Drag the mouse pointer down to the Transform category and then choose **Chevron Down**.

Now you will center all headings and format one of the headings.

12. Position the mouse pointer in the left margin area next to the WordArt object and then click and drag down to select the WordArt and the other two headings.

13. Choose **Home→Paragraph→Center** ☰.

14. Select *The Children's Clinic* and then choose **Home→Font→dialog box launcher** ⬜ to display the Font dialog box.

Ⓐ Choose **Calibri, Bold, 18 pt**.

Ⓑ In the Effects area, check **Small Caps**.

Ⓒ Click **OK**.

15. Save the file.

Inserting a Picture and Using Picture Effects

Including pictures in your documents can make them rich and colorful and enhance your message. In addition to accessing pictures online, you can also insert pictures directly from files. For example, you can insert a scanned picture or a picture taken with a digital camera and stored on your computer.

And Word has great picture effects that you can add to your images, such as shadows, reflections, glows, soft edges, bevels, and 3-D rotations.

≡ Insert→Illustrations→Pictures 🖼

≡ Picture Tools→Format→Picture Styles→Picture Effects ▣

DEVELOP YOUR SKILLS: W6-D2

In this exercise, you will insert and crop a graphic image. Then you will add a picture effect to the image.

1. Save your file as **W6-D2-RaritanNewsltr**.
2. Position the insertion point on the blank line below the date.
3. Choose **Insert→Illustrations→Pictures** 🖼.
4. Navigate to your **Word Chapter 6** folder and double-click the **W6-D2-RaritanClinic.png** graphics file to insert it.

   Next you will crop the words off of the image.
5. With the picture selected, choose **Picture Tools→Format→Size→Crop** 🖼.
6. Position the mouse pointer on the right-center cropping handle and drag left to crop off the words *Raritan Clinic East*.
7. Position the mouse pointer on the bottom-center cropping handle and drag up to remove the words at the bottom of the image, and then click in the document to finish cropping.
8. If necessary, choose **View→Show→Ruler** and then resize the image from a corner sizing handle, making it approximately **1½" wide**.
9. With the image selected, choose **Picture Tools→Format→Picture Styles→Picture Effects** ▣.
10. Drag the mouse pointer to the **Shadow** category, and in the Outer category choose **Offset Diagonal Bottom Right**.
11. Choose **Home→Paragraph→Center** ≡.
12. Save the file.

Inserting a Section Break and Setting Up Columns

Whenever you have a page-oriented formatting change that affects only part of a document, such as margins, page orientation, or columns, you need to set off that part with a section break. You use a Continuous break to start a new section within a page. You use a Next Page section break to start a new section on a new page, or, if your document is laid out in a book-like format, you can specify that the section break should start on an Even Page or Odd Page.

When you set a document or a section of a document in columns, you can choose preset formats or set up your own column width and spacing.

≡ Layout→Page Setup→Breaks 🗒

≡ Layout→Page Setup→Columns 🗔

In this exercise, you will insert a section break and lay out the newsletter in columns. Then you will customize the column layout.

1. Save your file as **W6-D3-RaritanNewsltr**.

2. Position the insertion point on the second blank line below the picture object.

3. Choose **Layout→Page Setup→Breaks** 🖽**→Continuous**.

4. Position the insertion point anywhere above the section break.

5. Choose **Layout→Page Setup→Columns** 🔳 and notice that one column is highlighted.

   Whenever text or images span the width of the page between the margins, it is considered one column.

6. Position the insertion point below the section break.

Add Newsletter Text and Customize Columns

7. Choose **Insert→Text→Object** ⬜ **menu button ▾→Text from File**.

8. Navigate to your **Word Chapter 6** folder and double-click **W6-D3-NewsltrTxt**.

9. Choose **Layout→Page Setup→Columns** 🔳 and then choose **More Columns** to open the Columns dialog box.

10. Follow these steps to customize the columns:

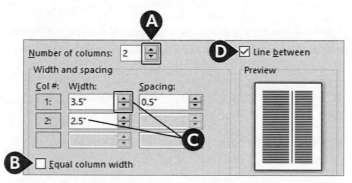

   Ⓐ Use the spin box to change the number of columns to **2**.

   Ⓑ Remove the checkmark from this checkbox.

   Ⓒ Use the spin box to change the width of column 1 to **3.5"** and notice that column 2 resizes automatically.

   Ⓓ Place a checkmark in the **Line Between** box to add a line between your columns.

11. Click **OK** and then scroll through the document to see the effect.

   The columns don't really look good this way. While you could click Undo, if you were to change your mind at a later time, there is still a quick way to return the columns back to equal size.

12. Choose **Layout→Page Setup→Columns** 🔳**→More Columns**.

13. Click the **Equal Column Width** checkbox and click **OK**.

14. Scroll through the document to see how it looks.

15. Save the file.

Artistic Effects and Wrapping Text Around a Picture

There are many tools on the contextual Format tab that allow you to customize images. Artistic effects can take your image styling to the next level. Some effects represent the image in pencil, paint, and various textures.

☰ Picture Tools→Format→Adjust→Artistic Effects 🖼

DEVELOP YOUR SKILLS: W6-D4

In this exercise, you will insert a picture and apply an artistic effect as well as a picture style to it. Then you will use the Layout Options smart tag to wrap text around the picture and you will balance the columns at the end of the newsletter.

1. Save your file as **W6-D4-RaritanNewsltr**.
2. Position the insertion point on page 2 to the left of the heading *The New Vaccine*.
3. Choose **Insert→Illustrations→Pictures** 🖼.
4. Navigate to your **Word Chapter 6** folder and double-click **W6-D4-VaccinePic.jpg** to insert the picture in the newsletter.
5. Resize the picture using a corner handle until it is about **1½" wide**.

Apply an Artistic Effect and a Picture Style

6. With the picture selected, choose **Picture Tools→Format→Adjust→Artistic Effects** 🖼 and then choose **Crisscross Etching**.
7. Choose **Picture Tools→Format→Picture Styles→More** ▾ button on the Picture Styles gallery.
8. Use Live Preview to sample various styles and then choose **Simple Frame, Black**.

Wrap Text Around a Picture

9. With the picture selected, click the **Layout Options** smart tag and choose the **Tight** text wrapping option.

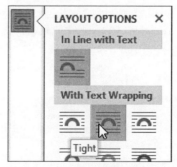

10. Click in the document to close the Layout Options gallery.

    Now you will balance the columns on page 2.

    You don't have to insert column breaks and move text around to balance columns. Inserting a Continuous section break at the end of the columns you want to balance is a quick trick for accomplishing the task.

11. Position the insertion point after the period following *disease* at the end of page 2.
12. Choose **Layout→Page Setup→Breaks** ⊞ →**Continuous**.
13. Save your file.

Inserting Cover Pages

A cover page catches a reader's eye as the first dynamic part of your document. You can easily add professional polish to a document by using a built-in cover page. There are a number of predesigned cover pages for you to choose from. And, if desired, you can modify the color and other design elements to achieve a cover page that best suits your needs.

≡ Insert→Pages→Cover Page 📄

DEVELOP YOUR SKILLS: W6-D5

In this exercise, you will add a cover page to your newsletter. Then you will add text to two text controls and delete text controls that you do not need.

1. Save your file as **W6-D5-RaritanNewsltr**.
2. Choose **Insert→Pages→Cover Page** 📄, scroll through the gallery of available options, and choose **Banded**.
3. Click the **Document Title** control and type **Raritan Clinic East Newsletter**

   The text wraps automatically within the control.

   Now you will repurpose one of the controls and delete controls you don't need.
4. Scroll to the bottom of the page, click the **Author** control (it may contain a person's name), and type **November, 2016**.
5. Click the **COMPANY NAME** control, click the **Company** tab at the top to select the entire control, and then tap ⌷Delete⌷.
6. Use the same technique to delete the **Company Address** control.
7. Save the file.

Printing Part of a Document

Sometimes you may want to print only part of a longer document—maybe a page or two or even just a couple of paragraphs. This can save both time and supplies. There are several techniques that make this an easy task, and they are found in the Print screen in Backstage view.

Custom Print options allow you to stipulate specific pages to print.

CUSTOM PRINT OPTIONS	
Print Consecutive Pages	Enter the page number of the first page to print, type a hyphen, and then type the page number of the last page to print.
Print Non-Consecutive Pages and Ranges	Enter the page numbers you want to print separated by commas (for example: 3,5,7,10-15).
Print a block of text	Select the text to print. Navigate to the Print screen in Backstage view. Choose Print Selection from the drop-down list.

≡ File→Print

DEVELOP YOUR SKILLS: W6-D6

In this exercise, you will explore options for printing part of a document. You will see how to print consecutive and nonconsecutive pages as well as a block of selected text.

1. Choose **File→Print** to display the Print screen in Backstage view.

   In the Settings part of the screen, notice that Print All Pages is the default.

2. Click the drop-down arrow next to Print All Pages.

3. Follow these steps to review the printing options:

   Settings

   Print All Pages
   The whole thing ▼

   Document

   Print All Pages
   The whole thing

   Print Selection ◀ **A**
   Just what you selected

   Print Current Page ◀ **B**
   Just this page

   Custom Print ◀ **C**
   Type specific pages, sections or ranges

   A This option is available only when you select text prior to accessing the Print screen.

   B This choice prints the page where the insertion point is located.

   C This option allows you to specify printing only certain pages.

4. Click the drop-down arrow to close the menu.

 You can specify which custom pages to print in the Pages field without opening the menu. When you begin entering page numbers, the setting automatically switches to Custom Print.

5. If you want to stay green and not print, click the **Back** ← button or print to PDF (you can make that choice in the Printer drop-down list).

6. Save the file and exit Word.

Self-Assessment

 Check your knowledge of this chapter's key concepts and skills using the Self-Assessment in your ebook or eLab course.

Reinforce Your Skills

Publish a Schoolyard Habitat Newsletter

Children who live in cities often miss out on the joys of the countryside. Kids for Change is seeking volunteers to help set up schoolyard habitats where children can experience firsthand the fun of creating their own gardens. In this exercise, you will create a newsletter with a section break and columns, and you will work with graphic images.

1. Start Word; create a new, blank document; and save it in your **Word Chapter 6** folder as **W6-R1-SchoolHabitat**.

2. If necessary, display formatting marks; then type these lines at the top of the document:
   Schoolyard Habitat
   Kids for Change

3. Tap Enter three times and then choose **Layout→Page Setup→Breaks ⊟→Continuous**.
   Next you will apply a WordArt format to Schoolyard Habitat.

4. Select the *Schoolyard Habitat* heading but not the paragraph symbol at the end of the line.

5. Choose **Insert→Text→WordArt** 4 and then choose **Fill — Blue, Accent 1, Shadow**.
   Next you will use the Layout Options smart tag to position the second line below the WordArt image.

6. With the WordArt object selected, click the smart tag and choose **In Line with Text**.

7. If necessary, click the border of the image to select the entire image.

8. Choose **Drawing Tools→Format→WordArt Styles→Text Effects** A and then slide the mouse pointer down to **Glow**.

9. In the Glow Variations section, choose **Green, 11 pt Glow, Accent Color 6**.

10. Choose **Drawing Tools→Format→WordArt Styles→Text Fill menu button** ▾ and then choose **Green, Accent 6, Darker 25%**.

11. Position the mouse pointer in the margin area to the left of the WordArt image and drag down to select it and the *Kids for Change* line.

12. Choose **Home→Paragraph→Center**.

13. Format the text *Kids for Change* with **Comic Sans MS, Bold, 16 pt** font.

14. Position the insertion point on the paragraph symbol below the section break.

15. Choose **Insert→Text→Object** ▢ **menu button** ▾ and choose **Text from File**.

16. Navigate to your **Word Chapter 6** folder and insert **W6-R1-HabitatContent**.

17. Position the insertion point on the second blank line below the text you just inserted.

18. Choose **Layout→Page Setup→Breaks→Continuous**.

19. Position the insertion point on the second blank line below the second section break.

Insert, Size, and Format a Picture

20. If necessary, choose **View→Show→Ruler**.

21. Choose **Insert→Illustrations→Pictures** and double-click the **W6-R1-Butterfly.jpg** picture to insert it.

22. With the picture selected, position the mouse pointer on the upper-right sizing handle and resize the picture to approximately **1" wide**.

23. Choose **Picture Tools→Format→Picture Styles**, click the **More** ⊡ button on the Picture Styles gallery, and then choose **Reflected Rounded Rectangle**.

24. Choose **Home→Paragraph→Center**.

Apply Columns

25. Position the insertion point anywhere in section 2.

26. Choose **Layout→Page Setup→Columns→More Columns**.

27. Choose **Two** in the Presets area, place a checkmark in the **Line Between** checkbox, and click **OK**.

The Habitat Team *heading should be moved to the top of the second column.*

28. Position the insertion point in front of the heading at the bottom of the first column.

29. Choose **Layout→Page Setup→Breaks→Column**.

30. Choose **File→Print** to preview the document and then click the **Back** ⊖ button to return to the Word screen.

31. Save and close the file.

REINFORCE YOUR SKILLS: W6-R2

Add Pizazz to a Wetlands Protection Newsletter

Kids for Change is starting a wetlands protection project. It is sending out a newsletter discussing the importance of wetlands and is seeking volunteers to become part of the project. In this exercise, you will insert a picture in the newsletter, apply artistic effects, and wrap text around the picture. You will add a cover page and print part of the newsletter.

1. Open **W6-R2-Wetlands** from your **Word Chapter 6** folder and save it as **W6-R2-WetlandsRevised**.

2. In the *Wetlands Are Busy Places* paragraph, position the insertion point at the beginning of the third sentence (begins with Wetlands).

3. Choose **Insert→Illustrations→Pictures** 🖼, navigate to your **Word Chapter 6** folder, and double-click **W6-R2-WetlandsPic.png**.

4. If necessary, turn on the ruler; then resize the picture from a corner handle until it is about **2" wide**.

5. Click the **Layout Options** smart tag, choose **Tight**, and then click in the document to close the gallery.

6. Click the picture border and choose **Picture Tools→Format→Adjust→Artistic Effects** 🖼 **→ Plastic Wrap**.

   Next, you will balance the columns.

7. Position the insertion point at the end of the right-hand column.

8. Choose **Layout→Page Setup→Breaks→Continuous**.

   Now you will add a cover page to the newsletter and you will print only the second page of the document.

9. Choose **Insert→Pages→Cover Page** 📄 **→Whisp**.

10. Click the **Document Title** control and type `Wetlands`.

11. If necessary, click the **Document Subtitle** control and type `Why They Are Important`.

12. Scroll to the bottom of the cover page, click the **Author Name** control, and type `Roger Washington`.

13. Click the **Company Name** control, click directly on the **Company** tab, and tap `Delete`.

14. Use the same technique to delete the **Date** control at the top of the cover page.

15. Choose **File→Print**; then click **Print All Pages** and choose **Print Current Page**.

16. Click the **Print** button, if desired, choosing to print to paper or PDF; otherwise, click the **Back** ⊖ button to return to the Word window.

17. Save and close the file.

REINFORCE YOUR SKILLS: W6-R3

Create a Newsletter to Fight Water Pollution

Kids for Change is starting a Protect Our Waterways project to fight water pollution. The supervisor for the project is using a newsletter as a means of getting the word out. In this exercise, you will set a document in newsletter columns and work with graphics.

1. Open **W6-R3-WaterPollution** from your **Word Chapter 6** folder and save it as **W6-R3-WaterPollutionRevised**.

2. If necessary, display formatting marks; then position the insertion point on the second paragraph symbol below the heading at the top of the document.

3. Choose **Layout→Page Setup→Breaks→Continuous**.

4. Select the heading at the top of the document but not the paragraph symbol at the end of the line.

5. Choose **Insert→Text→WordArt** 🄰 and then choose **Fill – Blue, Accent 5, Outline – Background 1, Hard Shadow – Accent 5**.

6. With the WordArt object selected, click the **Layout Options** smart tag and choose the **Top and Bottom** layout.

7. Click in the document to close the gallery and then click the border of the WordArt object.

8. Choose **Drawing Tools→Format→WordArt Styles→Text Effects** 🄰 and slide the mouse pointer down to **Transform**.

9. Choose **Square** in the Warp category.

10. Position the insertion point on the WordArt border and drag to the right to center the object between the margins.

Use Font Effects and Insert a Picture

11. Select the *Water Pollution* heading in the body of the document.

12. Choose **Home→Font→dialog box launcher** ⌐ and then check **Small Caps** in the Effects section and click **OK**.

13. Choose **Home→Clipboard** and double-click **Format Painter**.

    Double-click the Format Painter when you want to copy a format to multiple text blocks.

14. Use the **Format Painter** to apply **Small Caps** to the other headings.

15. Click the **Format Painter** again to turn it off.

16. Position the insertion point on the second blank line below the last paragraph.

17. Choose **Insert→Illustrations→Pictures**, navigate to your **Word Chapter 6** folder, and double-click **W6-R3-FishingPic.jpg**.

18. If necessary, turn on the ruler; then resize the picture from a corner handle until it is about **2½" wide**.

19. Choose **Picture Tools→Format→Picture Effects** ▣ **→Soft Edges** and then choose **10 Point**.

Apply and Balance Columns

20. Click the insertion point in the body of the document.

21. Choose **Layout→Page Setup→Columns** ▤ **→More Columns**.

22. Choose **Two** in the Presets area, check the **Line Between** checkbox, and then click **OK**.

23. Delete the paragraph symbol at the top of the left-hand column.

24. Position the insertion point on the last paragraph symbol at the bottom of the right-hand column.

25. Choose **Layout→Page Setup→Breaks→Continuous**.

26. Select the picture and choose **Home→Paragraph→Center**.

Add a Cover Page

27. Choose **Insert→Pages→Cover Page** and choose **Grid**.

28. Click the **Document Title** control and type **Let's Fight Water Pollution**, and the text will automatically wrap.

29. Delete the other text controls on the page.

30. Save and close the file.

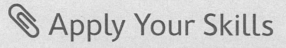 Apply Your Skills

Publish a Travel Newsletter

Universal Corporate Events keeps its clients informed about the latest travel industry news by publishing a monthly newsletter. In this exercise, you will create a newsletter in column format and with graphic images.

1. Open **W6-A1-CorpTravel** from your **Word Chapter 6** folder and save it as **W6-A1-CorpTravelRevised**.

2. If necessary, display formatting marks; then position the insertion point on the second blank line below the *Meeting and Event Planning Services* heading and insert a **Continuous** section break.

3. Select the first heading (Universal Corporate Events) but not the paragraph symbol at the end of the line.

4. Apply **WordArt** to the first line heading using **Fill – Gray-50%, Accent 3, Sharp Bevel**.

5. Use the **Layout Options** smart tag to apply **Top and Bottom** text wrapping.

6. Apply the **Square** text effect in the Warp section of the **Transform** category to the WordArt object.

7. Choose **Drawing Tools→Format→WordArt Styles→Text Fill menu button ▼** and then choose **Blue, Accent 5, Lighter 40%**.

8. Format the second heading line, *Meeting and Event Planning Services*, with **Tahoma 14 pt** font.

9. Center both heading lines. (Drag the WordArt object to center it.)

10. Position the insertion point at the beginning of the first subheading.

11. Tap Enter and then position the insertion point on the blank line.

Insert and Format Pictures

12. Insert the **W6-A1-HappyPic.png** and resize it to **1" wide**.

13. With the image selected, choose **Picture Tools→Format→Picture Styles→Picture Effects→Glow** and then choose **Gold, 8 pt glow, Accent color 4**.

14. Position the insertion point at the beginning of the *Avis Budget Reports* heading on page 2.

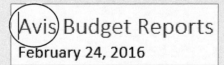

15. Tap Enter and then position the insertion point on the blank line.

16. Insert **W6-A1-RentalPic.jpg** and resize it to **2" wide**.

17. Open the **Picture Styles** gallery and choose **Soft Edge Oval**.

18. Position the insertion point in the body of the document; format the document in an equal-width, two-column layout, with a line between the columns.

   The Better Direction heading at the bottom of the right-hand column on page 1 would look better at the top of the next column.

19. Position the insertion point in front of the *4* and then choose **Layout→Page Setup→Breaks→ Column**.

   There are two lines flowing onto the last page, and it would look better if they were on page 2. Resizing the rental picture might solve the issue.

20. Resize the picture to **1½"** or the size needed to make the lines flow to page 2.

21. Save and close the file.

APPLY YOUR SKILLS: W6-A2

Create a Bleisure Newsletter

This month's Universal Corporate Events newsletter focuses on the latest "bleisure" (a blend of business and leisure) travel trend. In this exercise, you will create a two-column newsletter, with a cover page and images, that is designed to keep clients' travel agents updated with the latest developments in the travel industry.

1. Open **W6-A2-BleisureTravel** from your **Word Chapter 6** folder and save it as **W6-A2-BleisureTravelRevised**.

2. If necessary, display formatting marks; then position the insertion point at the end of the heading, *The Bleisure Trend,* and tap Enter twice.

3. With the insertion point on the second blank line, insert a **Continuous** section break.

4. Select the heading, *The Bleisure Trend*, but not the paragraph symbol and apply the WordArt style **Fill – Blue, Accent 1, Shadow**.

5. Open the **Layout Options** smart tag and apply **Top and Bottom** wrapping.

6. Select the WordArt object, choose **Drawing Tools→Format→WordArt Styles→Text Effects→Shadow**, and from the Outer category, apply the **Offset Diagonal Top Right** style.

7. Drag the WordArt to the right to center it between the margins.

8. Using the Font dialog box, format the *Introduction* heading with **14 pt** font size and **Small Caps**.

9. Use the **Format Painter** to apply the same format to the other headings in the document.

10. With the insertion point in the body of the document, format the section with two equal-width columns and a line between the columns.

Add a Picture and a Cover Page

11. Position the insertion point in front of the paragraph beginning, *In fact*, on page 1.

   In fact, according to a
   Hospitality report, 60
   reported having taken

12. Insert the picture file **W6-A2-BleisurePic.jpg** and then resize it to **1½" wide**.

13. Click the **Layout Options** smart tag and choose **Tight** wrapping.

14. Delete the extra paragraph symbol at the top of the left-hand column.

    There are just a few lines flowing onto the second page. Next, you will narrow the margins to make the document fit on one page.

15. Choose **Layout→Page Setup→Margins** and then choose the preset **Narrow** option.

    Now you will finish off the newsletter with a cover page.

16. Insert a cover page using the **Slice (Dark)** option.

17. Click the **Document Title** control and type `Universal Corporate Events`.

18. Click the **Document Subtitle** and type `Bleisure Travel`.

19. Save and close the file.

Create a Travel Tips Newsletter

Universal Corporate Events shares travel tips with its clients' travel agents in this month's newsletter. In this exercise, you will publish a two-column travel tips newsletter incorporating WordArt, a picture, and a cover page.

1. Open **W6-A3-TravelTips** from your **Word Chapter 6** folder and save it as **W6-A3-TravelTipsRevised**.

2. Select *Universal Corporate Events* at the top of the document but not the paragraph symbol at the end of the line.

3. Apply the WordArt style **Fill, White — Outline — Accent 1, Glow — Accent 1**.

4. Choose **Drawing Tools→Format→WordArt Styles→Text Effects**, and in the **Reflection** category, choose **Tight Reflection, Touching**.

5. Open the **Layout Options** smart tag, choose **Top and Bottom**, and then drag the WordArt object to the right to center it between the margins.

6. Position the insertion point on the second paragraph symbol below the WordArt heading and insert a **Continuous** section break.

7. Position the insertion point in the body of the document and format the text in two columns.

8. Delete the paragraph symbol at the top of the left-hand column.

9. Position the insertion point at the end of the right-hand column, tap Enter , and insert the picture **W6-A3-AirportPic.png**.

10. Resize the picture so it is even with the bottom of the left-hand column.

11. Choose **Picture Tools→Format→Picture Styles→Picture Border menu button** ▾ and then choose **Blue, Accent 5, Lighter 40%**.

12. Click the **Picture Border menu button** ▾ again, choose **3 pt** from the **Weight** menu, and then center the image within the column.

13. Insert the **Slice (Light)** cover page.

14. Edit the controls as indicated:
    - Document Title control: **Travel Tips**
    - Document Subtitle control: **Universal Corporate Events**

15. Click the **School** control at the bottom of the page and notice the School and Course Title controls are inside a rectangle shape.

16. Click the border of the rectangle to select everything inside it and tap $\boxed{\text{Delete}}$.

17. Save and close the file; exit Word.

Extend Your Skills

These exercises challenge you to think critically and apply your new skills. You will be evaluated on your ability to follow directions, completeness, creativity, and the use of proper grammar and mechanics. Save files to your chapter folder. Submit assignments as directed.

W6-E1 That's the Way I See It

As a small-business owner, you want to keep your customers interested in what you're doing, so you decide to send out monthly newsletters. Determine the type of business you own and then place a WordArt object with your company's name at the top of a new document. The object should span the margins (one column). Conduct online research related to your type of business to find information you think will be of interest to your customers. Pull the information into your document, remembering to cite your sources. Lay out the document in newsletter-style columns. Insert an image that relates to the content and use a style from the Picture Styles gallery to enhance the image. Place headings within the newsletter and format them with Small Caps along with a font and font size of your choice. Add a cover page that blends well with your newsletter. Save your newsletter as **W6-E1-MyBiz**.

W6-E2 Be Your Own Boss

As the owner of Blue Jean Landscaping, you decide to keep in touch with customers by distributing a newsletter. Start a new document and save it as **W6-E2-Landscape**.

Place the company name at the top of the newsletter using a WordArt style. Insert a continuous section break after the WordArt. Search online for decorative plants and shrubs that can be used for landscaping. Pull in the results of your research as the primary content for the newsletter, ensuring you cite your sources. Format the text in newsletter-style columns. Insert a picture that reflects the newsletter content and apply a Picture Effect. Then insert headings in the document body and apply Small Caps and the font and point size of your choice. Add a cover page of your choice.

W6-E3 Demonstrate Proficiency

Stormy BBQ keeps its customers engaged through a monthly newsletter. This month's newsletter will describe the benefits of local farm-raised pork and beef. Conduct online research to gather the primary content for your newsletter, ensuring you cite your sources. Place the name of the business at the top of the newsletter formatting it with WordArt and then apply the Text Fill of your choice. Insert a section break to separate the WordArt from the main article. Format the newsletter in columns with a line between. Insert at least two pictures that enhance your message. Add headings within the newsletter, add the text effect of Small Caps or All Caps, and then apply the font and font size of your choice. Add a cover page that blends well with the newsletter. Save your file as **W6-E3-FarmRaised**.

7 | Working with Long Documents

Long documents are important in both academia and business and range in type from dissertations to research reports. In this chapter, you will use styles to provide consistent heading formatting, which leads the reader's eye through the document. You will customize styles and other features to suit your needs, and you will use several techniques to quickly navigate long documents. Finally, you will work with long tables to make them easy to read and to find information.

LEARNING OBJECTIVES

▸ Format with styles

▸ Create and manage custom styles

▸ Use themes and style sets

▸ Customize bullets and numbering

▸ Navigate long documents

▸ Format long tables

📁 Project: Reporting on Common Childhood Illnesses

Raritan Clinic East periodically hosts seminars for parents of young children to discuss common childhood illnesses. As a certified nursing assistant, you have been asked to research these illnesses and compile a report that the clinic will use as a handout for the seminars. You will use styles, themes, and other formatting features to make your report engaging to the reader. Then you will create a table to keep track of the attendees.

Formatting Text with Styles

A style is a collection of formats that you can apply to text. When you type a document, you are automatically using a style. This is typically the Normal style, which includes Calibri font, 11 pt, left-justified, and so forth. Or, you might be using a custom template that is set up with a different default style. Styles are based on the current template's theme, which is a set of colors, fonts, and graphic effects. Styles help you provide consistent formatting throughout a document.

The Styles gallery on the Ribbon is limited to frequently used styles. For a more in-depth approach and access to more styles, you must open the Styles task pane.

> ⚠️ View the video "The Styles Gallery and the Styles Task Pane."

> ☰ Home→Styles→dialog box launcher 🔲

Custom Styles

Thus far, you have used Word's built-in styles. However, there may be situations in which the built-in styles do not meet your needs. For example, Raritan Clinic East has formatting standards set for different types of documents. You can create custom styles to meet those standards.

There are two approaches you can take to create custom styles. The method you choose is a matter of personal preference; both are equally effective.

▸ **Style by definition:** Choose all formats from the Create New Style from Formatting dialog box.

▸ **Style by example:** Format a block of text with the formats you wish to include in your style. The Create New Style from Formatting dialog box can copy the formats from your formatted text.

> ⚠️ View the video "Create a Style by Definition and a Style by Example."

DEVELOP YOUR SKILLS: W7-D1

In this exercise, you will create custom styles. You'll begin by opening the Styles task pane and creating a new style by example for the document heading. Then you will create a style by definition.

1. Start Word, open **W7-D1-SickKids** from your **Word Chapter 7** folder, and save it as **W7-D1-SickKidsRevised**.

2. Select the *Raritan Clinic East* heading at the top of the document.

   Now you will apply the example formatting.

3. Choose **Home→Font→Font menu button** ▾ and then choose **Tahoma** from the menu.

4. Click the **Font Size menu** button ▾ and choose **24 pt**.

5. Choose **Home→Paragraph→Center** ▤.

6. Choose **Home→Styles→dialog box launcher** ⬒ to display the Styles task pane.

7. At the bottom of the task pane, click the **New Style** ⬒ button to open the Create New Style from Formatting dialog box.

8. Follow these steps to complete the new style:

Ⓐ Notice the example formatting that you applied earlier.

Ⓑ Name the style **Doc Head**.

Ⓒ Make sure the Style Type is **Paragraph**.

Ⓓ If necessary, set the new style to be based on the **Normal** style and the formatting for the following paragraph to **Normal**.

9. At the bottom of the dialog box, make sure the **Add to the Styles Gallery** box is checked and then click **OK**.

When the text that has the style applied is selected or the insertion point is in the text, your new style is highlighted in the Styles gallery on the Ribbon and in the Styles task pane.

Create Styles by Definition

Now you'll create a style by definition for the subheading at the top of the document.

10. Click in the *Childhood Diseases Seminar* subheading.

11. Click the **New Style** button at the bottom of the Styles task pane.

12. Set up the top portion of the dialog box as shown.

Properties	
<u>N</u>ame:	Subhead 1
Style <u>t</u>ype:	Paragraph
Style <u>b</u>ased on:	¶ Normal
<u>S</u>tyle for following paragraph:	¶ Normal

You could do some font formatting in this dialog box, but you will choose the Format button instead because it provides more font options.

13. Click the **Format** button at the bottom of the dialog box, choose **Font** to open the Font dialog box, and then choose **Tahoma** from the Font list.

Tip! *If you type a* t *in the field at the top of the font list, the list automatically scrolls to the Ts.*

14. Choose **14 pt** as the font size, check the **Small Caps** checkbox, and then click **OK**.

Your font choices appear in the dialog box, and the preview screen displays the effect of your choices. Next you will center the subheading, and you can do that here in this dialog box.

15. Click the **Center** button in the paragraph alignment group and then click **OK**.

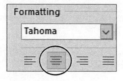

The new style appears in the Styles gallery on the Ribbon and in the Styles task pane.

Now you will create styles for the subheadings in the body of the document. You will have two levels of subheadings, and you will create styles by example for these subheadings.

16. In the next line, select *WebMD* and format it with **Arial, 14 pt**.

17. Click the **New Style** button and follow these guidelines to finish creating the style:
- Name: **Subhead 2**
- Style Type: **Paragraph**
- Style Based On: **Normal**
- Style for Following Paragraph: **Normal**

18. Notice the example font formatting you applied in the Formatting area of the dialog box and then click **OK**.

You will apply the Subhead 2 style to another subheading in the document.

19. Scroll to page 3, position the insertion point in the subheading *Parents.com*, and choose **Subhead 2** from the Styles gallery.

20. Scroll back up to page 1, position the insertion point in the *RSV* subheading, and choose **Home→Font**.

21. Choose the **Arial** font and the **12 pt** font size.

22. Click the **New Style** ⧉ button and follow these guidelines to finish creating the style:
    - Name: **Subhead 3**
    - Style Type: **Paragraph**
    - Style Based On: **Normal**
    - Style for Following Paragraph: **Normal**

23. Notice the example settings in the Formatting area and then click **OK**.

    Now you will apply Subhead 3 to the rest of the subheadings in the document.

24. Click in the *Ear Infection* subheading and choose **Subhead 3** from the Styles task pane.

25. Use the same technique to apply Subhead 3 to the remaining subheadings:
    - Glue Ear
    - Croup
    - Hand-Foot-and-Mouth Disease
    - Pinkeye
    - Fifth Disease
    - Common Cold
    - Strep Throat
    - Influenza
    - Symptoms You Should Never Ignore

26. Save the file.

Modifying Styles and Clearing All Formatting

You can modify a built-in style as well as styles that you create. Modifying styles can help you maintain consistency when you make formatting changes and can speed up that process. You can make global formatting changes by modifying a style. When you change a style, the change is applied to all the text in the current document that is formatted with the style. This eliminates the need to modify each text block individually—a big time saver.

There may be times when it is easier to reformat text from the beginning rather than trying to figure out which formats were used. This can be particularly helpful if you've inherited a heavily formatted document. The Clear All command in the Styles task pane is a quick way to remove styles and all other unwanted formatting from a document or a selected block of text.

DEVELOP YOUR SKILLS: W7-D2

In this exercise, you will modify the Subhead 3 style. When you do, you will see how it impacts all text formatted with that style. Then you will use the Clear All feature to remove formatting from a heading.

1. Save your file as **W7-D2-SickKidsRevised**.

2. Hover the mouse pointer over **Subhead 3** in the Styles task pane and click the drop-down arrow.

3. Choose **Modify** from the menu to open the Modify Style dialog box.

   This dialog box contains the same elements as the Create New Style from Formatting dialog box.

4. Click the **Italic** *I* button to add that format to the Subhead 3 style and then click **OK**.

5. Scroll through the document and notice that all the subheadings with the Subhead 3 style are now italicized.

   You've decided to reformat the heading at the top of the document. Because this style is used only once in the document, you will clear all the formatting and apply direct formatting to the heading.

6. Select the *Raritan Clinic East* heading at the top of the document, scroll to the top of the Styles task pane, and choose **Clear All**.

7. Click the **Font group dialog box launcher** ⌐ and then choose **Tahoma**, **22 pt**, **Small Caps** and click **OK**.

8. Choose **Home→Paragraph→Center** ≡.

   Notice that the Normal style is highlighted in the task pane. You applied direct formatting to text that is formatted with the Normal style.

9. Save the file.

Removing and Deleting Styles

You can remove a style from the Styles gallery on the Ribbon without removing it from the Styles task pane. Because the Styles gallery on the Ribbon is a quick way to get to styles, you should save it for just the styles you use frequently and not clutter it with styles that you don't often use or don't plan to use at all. You can leave the style in the task pane for future use, or, if you prefer, you can delete it from the task pane. Completely deleting a style removes its formatting from the document.

DEVELOP YOUR SKILLS: W7-D3

In this exercise, you will remove the Doc Head style from the Styles gallery and then delete it from the task pane.

1. Save your file as **W7-D3-SickKidsRevised**.

2. If the Doc Head style is not visible in the Styles gallery on the Ribbon, click the **More** ⊡ button to open the gallery and then locate the Doc Head style.

3. Right-click on the style name and choose **Remove from Styles Gallery**.

   Notice that Doc Head is still visible in the Styles task pane. You'll delete it next.

4. Hover the mouse pointer over Doc Head in the Styles task pane, click the drop-down arrow, and choose **Delete Doc Head**.

5. When the message appears verifying the deletion, click **Yes**.

   The style is deleted from the task pane.

6. Save and close your document.

Using Themes and Style Sets

Themes and style sets are document-level formatting features that can instantly add color and visual variety to your entire document. A theme is a combination of colors, fonts, and graphic elements that you can apply to any document. Style sets change font and paragraph properties. Themes and style sets create the biggest impact when you use built-in styles.

≡ Design→Document Formatting→Themes 🄰

≡ Design→Document Formatting→Style Sets gallery

Customizing a Theme

You can customize any theme to match your creative side. Changing a theme font changes any text formatted with fonts that have (Headings) or (Body) next to their names in the font list. Calibri Light (Heading) and Calibri (Body) are the theme fonts for the default Office theme. When you change the theme, the associated theme fonts change. You can also customize the theme color. Changing a theme color or font does not permanently change the built-in theme; it modifies only your current document.

DEVELOP YOUR SKILLS: W7-D4

In this exercise, you will use a different version of the Childhood Diseases Seminar handout. This version uses Word's built-in styles, and a cover page has been added. You will use Live Preview to examine a variety of themes and style sets, and you will also apply a new theme and style set to your report.

1. Open **W7-D4-SickKids** from your **Word Chapter 7** folder and save it as **W7-D4-SickKidsRevised**.

2. Scroll to page 1 of the main document and position the insertion point in the *Raritan Clinic East* heading.

   Notice that the built-in Title style is highlighted in the Styles task pane.

3. Position the insertion point in the *Childhood Diseases Seminar* subheading and see that the built-in Heading 1 style is active in the Styles task pane.

4. Examine the other headings, and you can see that built-in styles have been applied.

   Remember, themes and style sets are most effective when using the built-in styles.

5. Scroll up to the cover page and choose **Design→Document Formatting→Themes** [Aa] to display the Themes gallery.

6. Hover the mouse pointer over several different themes and observe the changes in your document.

7. Choose the **Frame** theme.

8. Scroll through the document to see the impact of the new theme.

   The built-in headings in the body of the document respond to a change in the theme.

Change the Theme Color and Font

9. Scroll so that the bottom of the cover page and the top of page 1 are both visible.

10. Choose **Design→Document Formatting→Colors** [■].

11. Use **Live Preview** to examine the different color schemes to see their effects and then choose **Blue Warm**.

12. Choose **Design→Document Formatting→Fonts** [>].

13. Use **Live Preview** to examine the font options and then choose **Franklin Gothic**.

Change the Style Set

14. Choose **Design→Document Formatting** and then click the **More** [▾] button to open the Style Sets gallery.

15. Use Live Preview to examine the different Style Sets and then choose **Centered**.

16. Scroll through the document to see the changes and then close the Styles task pane.

17. Save the file.

Customizing Bullet and Number Formats

The Bullets and Numbering libraries enable you to choose a different style for your bulleted or numbered list. You can also define your own custom formats. When working with long documents, you may want to adjust the formatting for certain lists as a visual cue that certain lists go together or should be considered separately.

 Remember that too much formatting can distract from your message. Less is more.

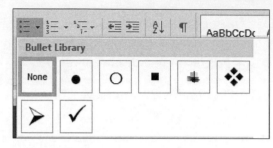

Bullet Library

Numbering Library

You can customize bullet styles by defining a symbol, picture, font, or alignment. You can customize the numbering style, font, format, and alignment.

Customize Bullet Format

Customize Number Format

≡ Home→Paragraph→Bullets

≡ Home→Paragraph→Numbering

DEVELOP YOUR SKILLS: W7-D5

In this exercise, you will choose a different bullet style from the Bullet Library. Then you will create a custom bullet using a symbol as the new bullet style.

1. Save your file as **W7-D5-SickKidsRevised**.

2. Scroll to page 4 and position the insertion point in the *Symptom #1* line.

3. Choose **Home**→**Paragraph**→**Bullets** menu button ▾ and choose the square bullet (location may vary).

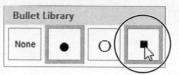

Notice that all the bullets in the list were updated. Next you will create a custom bullet.

4. Choose **Home**→**Paragraph**→**Bullets** menu button ▾ and choose **Define New Bullet**.

5. Follow these steps to define a symbol as a new bullet:

Ⓐ Click the **Symbol** button to open the Symbol dialog box.

Ⓑ Choose the **Wingdings** font.

Ⓒ Make sure the scroll box is at the top of the scroll bar, choose this symbol (location may vary), and then click **OK** twice.

Again, all of the bullets have changed to the custom bullet.

6. Choose **Home**→**Paragraph**→**Bullets** menu button ▾ to display the Bullet library.

The new bullet was added to the library. Now you'll remove the bullet so the next student who uses your computer will have the same experience.

7. Right-click the new bullet in the Bullet library area and choose **Remove**.

8. Display the Bullet Library again and notice that the new bullet was removed; close the menu.

9. Save your file.

Using Special Characters

Special characters appear in the Symbol dialog box. There is a variety of special characters, including nonbreaking hyphens or spaces. These characters allow you to keep terms together that should remain together on one line, such as dates, phone numbers, and names.

≡ Insert→Symbols→Symbol Ω→Special Characters

DEVELOP YOUR SKILLS: W7-D6

In this exercise, you will insert nonbreaking spaces in doctors' names that appear in the document. This will correct doctors' names that split across two lines, and it's also a safety measure in the event that future edits would cause the name to split across two lines.

1. Save your file as **W7-D6-SickKidsRevised**.

2. Scroll to page 3, locate the fifth line in the *Common Cold* paragraph, and position the insertion point after *Fred*.

> might lead to an overdose," says pediatrician F(red| Hirschenfang, M.D.,

3. Tap [Delete] to remove the space.

4. Choose **Insert→Symbols→Symbol** Ω and then choose **More Symbols** from the menu.

5. Click the **Special Characters** tab in the Symbol dialog box and choose **Nonbreaking Space**.

Symbols	Special Characters	
Character		**Shortcut key**
—	Em Dash	Alt+Ctrl+Num -
–	En Dash	Ctrl+Num -
-	Nonbreaking Hyphen	Ctrl+Shift+_
¬	Optional Hyphen	Ctrl+-
	Em Space	
	En Space	
	1/4 Em Space	
°	Nonbreaking Space	Ctrl+Shift+Space
©	Copyright	Alt+Ctrl+C
®	Registered	Alt+Ctrl+R

6. Click the **Insert** button at the bottom of the dialog box and then click **Close**.

7. Display the formatting marks to see the character that represents a nonbreaking space.

8. Position the insertion point after the comma following the last name and [Delete] the space.

9. Choose **Insert→Symbols→Symbol** Ω **→More Symbols**, click the **Special Characters** tab, and choose **Nonbreaking Space**.

   Notice the shortcut keystrokes for a nonbreaking space: [Ctrl]+[Shift]+[Space]. *You can use the keystrokes for the remaining two names.*

10. Click the **Insert** button and then click **Close**.

11. Scroll down to the sixth line in the next paragraph and notice the doctor's name that starts at the end of the line.

12. Position the insertion point after the *y* in *Jay* and tap [Delete].

13. Press [Ctrl]+[Shift]+[Space] to insert a nonbreaking space.

14. Use the same technique to replace the space following the comma after the last name with a nonbreaking space.

15. Locate *Dr. Hirschenfang's* name starting at the end of the sixth line in the *Influenza* paragraph and replace the space between *Dr.* and his last name with a nonbreaking space.

16. Save the file.

Navigating Long Documents

A long, complex document can be difficult to navigate. Fortunately, there are a number of helpful tools that make it easier. The Navigation pane provides several ways to move around a document, and bookmarks are useful if you frequently need to return to the same location in a document. If you want to compare two separate parts of the same document, using the Split Window feature is a great way to do so.

The Navigation Pane

The Navigation pane provides three primary methods for locating a search term in a document: headings, pages, and results.

The Pages option displays thumbnails of pages where the search term appears; clicking a thumbnail jumps the document to that page.

The Results option displays the search term in context; clicking one of the results jumps the document to that page.

Search terms are entered here.

The Headings option will list any heading styles in your document. If the search term appears within a heading, it will be highlighted. Click a heading to jump to that part of the document.

The arrows allow you to search up and down the document.

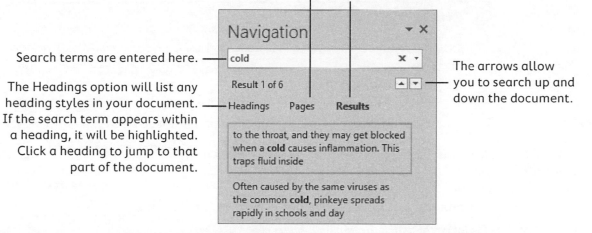

≡ View→Show→Navigation Pane | Ctrl+F

Navigating with Bookmarks

You can assign a bookmark name to text or other objects in a document. Once a bookmark is set up, you can easily navigate to it by choosing the desired bookmark name from the Bookmark dialog box.

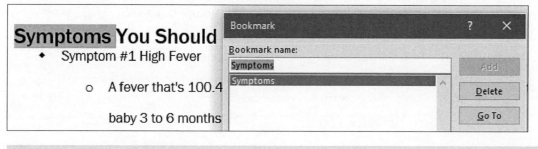

≡ Insert→Links→Bookmark

Splitting the Window

Imagine you want to check whether the executive summary of a report accurately reflects the report's content. Splitting the window is the answer. You can view the executive summary in one window and scroll through the rest of the document in the other window.

Childhood Diseases Seminar

WebMD

Split bar | Despite vaccines that have made many childhood diseases rare, many common illnesses continue to plague children. Following are descriptions of a few of these illnesses taken from the WebMD website.

cold-like symptoms before the rash is seen. Once the rash appears, the child is usually no longer contagious. Up to 20% of kids get it by age 5, and up to 60% have had it by age 19. The rash usually

☰ View→Window→Split ▦

DEVELOP YOUR SKILLS: W7-D7

In this exercise, you will navigate in a long document using several techniques: Navigation pane, bookmarks, and split window.

1. Save your file as **W7-D7-SickKidsRevised**.
2. Choose **View→Show→Navigation Pane** and enter **cold** as your search term.

Tip! *You can also open the Navigation pane by pressing* Ctrl + F .

3. Choose the Results option at the top of the Navigation pane, click the fourth result, **Common Cold**, and the document jumps to that location.

   Notice that the term is highlighted in yellow wherever it appears.

4. Click the **Headings** option at the top of the Navigation pane.

   If the document contains heading styles, they are listed here. The headings where the search term appears are highlighted in yellow.

5. Click the *Ear Infection* heading to jump to that part of the document and, again, the search term is highlighted in yellow.

6. Click the **Pages** option at the top of the pane to see thumbnails of the pages that contain the search term.

7. Click the second thumbnail to jump to that page.

8. Click the up and down arrows in the upper-right corner of the Navigation pane to scroll through all occurrences of the term.

9. Close ☒ the Navigation pane.

Use Bookmarks

10. Scroll to page 4 and select *Symptoms* in the heading titled *Symptoms You Should Never Ignore*.

11. Choose **Insert→Links→Bookmark** 🔖 and then type **Symptoms** in the Bookmark Name field and click **Add**.

Tip! *A bookmark name can be up to 40 characters, including letters and numbers, but it must begin with a letter and cannot contain spaces or symbols.*

12. Press $\boxed{\text{Ctrl}}$ + $\boxed{\text{Home}}$ or scroll up to move to the top of the document.

13. Choose **Insert→Links→Bookmark** 🔖.

14. *Symptoms* is already selected, so click **Go To** to jump to the bookmarked text and then click **Close**.

Split the Window

15. Choose **View→Window→Split** ⬜.

    A split bar appears across the window. Notice on the right-hand side of the screen that there are two scroll bars, one for the top window and one for the bottom window.

16. In the top window, scroll to the top of page 1 and, in the bottom window, scroll to the top of page 3.

    You can also split the window into different proportions, allowing more text to show on one side.

17. Position the mouse pointer on the split bar.

18. When the mouse pointer changes to a double-headed arrow, drag the split bar up about an inch.

19. Double-click the split bar to return to one window.

20. Save and close the file.

Large Tables

If you're working with large tables, making them user-friendly is important. It should be easy for the reader to scan a table and get information. If possible, columns should be wide enough to prevent text from wrapping within the cells. Adding white space within the table makes the text appear less dense. Repeating column headers from one page to the next is essential for the reader to understand the meaning of the data. Sizing a table to best fit the page adds to its readability.

≡ Table Tools→Layout→Cell Size→dialog box launcher ⌐

≡ Table Tools→Layout→Alignment→Cell Margins ⊞

DEVELOP YOUR SKILLS: W7-D8

In this exercise, you will modify a large table, making it easier to read by widening columns where text is wrapping, adding white space within cells, and repeating column headers from page to page. You'll also add a caption to the table.

1. Open **W7-D8-SeminarAttendees** from your **Word Chapter 7** folder and save it as **W7-D8-SeminarAttendeesRevised**.

    The text is wrapping in several columns, making it difficult to read. At the same time the table already spans the width of the page. Rotating this document to landscape (horizontal) orientation and changing the table width should solve the problem.

2. Choose **Layout→Page Setup→Orientation** 📄 and choose **Landscape** from the menu.

3. Choose **Table Tools→Layout→Cell Size→dialog box launcher** ⌐.

4. In the Table Properties dialog box, if necessary, click the **Table** tab.

5. Change Preferred Width to **9"** and then click **OK**.

   Adding white space within the cells will certainly add to the table's readability.

6. Choose **Table Tools→Layout→Alignment→Cell Margins** 🔲.

7. In the Table Options dialog box, change the top and bottom cell margins to **0.05** and then click **OK**.

8. If necessary, position the insertion point in the first row of the table.

   This is the row that will repeat at the top of each page.

9. Choose **Table Tools→Layout→Cell Size→dialog box launcher** 🔳 and click the **Row** tab.

10. Place a checkmark in the **Repeat as Header Row at the Top of Each Page** checkbox and then click **OK**.

11. Scroll down to see the header row at the top of page 2.

    Now you will add a caption to the table.

12. Choose **References→Captions→Insert Caption** 🔳 and then click the **New Label** button toward the bottom of the dialog box.

13. In the New Label dialog box, type `Childhood Diseases Seminar Attendees` and click **OK**; click **OK** again to close the Caption dialog box.

14. Scroll to the bottom of the document to see the caption.

    Captions are typically numbered, but because this is the only table in the document, numbering is not necessary.

15. Position the insertion point at the end of the caption and then tap ⟨Backspace⟩ twice to delete the number.

16. Save and close the file; exit Word.

Self-Assessment

 Check your knowledge of this chapter's key concepts and skills using the Self-Assessment in your ebook or eLab course.

⚲ Reinforce Your Skills

REINFORCE YOUR SKILLS: W7-R1

Create a New Members Handout

Kids for Change wants new members to understand the importance of its motto, Think Globally, Act Locally. One of the members researched the origins of the phrase, and now you've been asked to format the document to make it more engaging. In this exercise, you will use styles, themes, and style sets to add appeal. You will begin by testing several different styles to see what you like best.

1. Start **Word**; open **W7-R1-GlobalLocal** from your **Word Chapter 7** folder and save it as **W7-R1-GlobalLocalRevised**.

2. Position the insertion point in *Introduction* at the top of page 1.

   You will apply a built-in style first.

3. Choose **Home→Styles** and in the Styles gallery on the Ribbon choose **Heading 1**.

   Now you will create a style by example.

4. Select the *Definition* heading for the next paragraph.

5. Choose **Home→Font→dialog box launcher** 🗗.

6. In the Font dialog box, choose **Arial Black**, **14 pt**, and **Small Caps**, and then click **OK**.

7. Choose **Home→Font→Font Color menu button** ▾ and choose **Orange, Accent 2, Darker 25%** from the color pallet.

8. Choose **Home→Styles→dialog box launcher** 🗗.

9. Click the **New Style** 🏄 button at bottom of the task pane.

10. Complete the information at the top of the dialog box as follows:
    - Name: **MyStyle1**
    - Style Type: **Paragraph**
    - Style Based On: **Normal**
    - Style for Following Paragraph: **Normal**

    Notice that your formatting has been copied into the Formatting area of the dialog box.

11. If necessary, click the **Add to the Styles Gallery** checkbox and click **OK**.

    The style name now appears in the Styles gallery on the Ribbon and in the Styles task pane. Next you will create a style by definition.

12. Scroll down and position the insertion point in the heading, *Origin in Town Planning*.

13. Click the **New Style** 🏄 button at the bottom of the task pane.

14. Complete the information at the top of the dialog box as follows:
    - Name: **MyStyle2**
    - Style Type: **Paragraph**
    - Style Based On: **Normal**
    - Style for Following Paragraph: **Normal**

15. In the Formatting area, choose **Century Schoolbook**, **14 pt**, and center alignment, and then click **OK**.

16. Scroll down and position the insertion point in the heading for the last paragraph, *Origins of the Phrase*, and apply the built-in **Heading 2** style.

Modify a Style

After scanning the different styles, you've decided to modify the Heading 1 style.

17. Position the insertion point in the *Introduction* heading at the top of page 1.

18. Hover the mouse pointer over the **Heading 1** style in the Styles task pane, click the drop-down arrow, and choose **Modify**.

19. Click the **Format** button at the bottom of the dialog box and choose **Font**.

20. Choose **Bold** in the Font Style field, click the drop-down arrow in the **Font Color** field, and choose **Green, Accent 6, Darker 25%**.

21. Check the **Small Caps** checkbox and then click **OK**.

22. In the Formatting area of the Modify Style dialog box, click the **Center** button and then click **OK**.

    Notice that the modifications you made are reflected in the style name in the Styles gallery. Now you need to decide on a style for the subheadings. You will modify the Heading 2 style.

23. Scroll to the last page and click in the heading, *Origins of the Phrase*. Hover the mouse pointer over **Heading 2** in the Styles task pane, click the drop-down arrow, and choose **Modify**.

24. In the Formatting area, click the **Bold** button, click the drop-down arrow in the color field and choose **Green, Accent 6, Darker 25%**, and then click **OK**.

    You are happy with the Heading 2 style, so now you'll apply it to the other subheadings.

25. Scroll up and position the insertion point in the heading, *Origin in Town Planning*, and then click the **Heading 2** style in the Styles task pane.

26. Scroll up and position the insertion point in the *Definition* heading and then apply the **Heading 2** style.

    Now you will investigate formats further using themes and style sets.

27. If necessary, scroll so the *Introduction* heading is at the top of the screen.

28. Choose **Design→Document Formatting→Themes** [Aa], use Live Preview to examine different Themes, and then choose **Slate** from the gallery.

29. Scroll up to the cover page to see the effect of the new theme.

30. Scroll back to page 1 and position the *Introduction* heading toward the middle of the screen.

31. Choose **Design→Document Formatting** and then click the **More** [▾] button from the Style Sets gallery.

32. Use Live Preview to view the effects of several Style Sets and then choose **Lines (Simple)**.

    Because you won't be using MyStyle1 and MyStyle2, you will delete them from the Styles task pane.

33. Hover the mouse pointer over **MyStyle1** in the task pane, click the drop-down arrow, and choose **Delete MyStyle1**.

34. When the message appears confirming the deletion, click **Yes**.

    The style was also removed from the Styles gallery on the Ribbon.

35. Use the same technique to delete **MyStyle2**.

36. Close the Styles task pane and then save and close the file.

Help Kids Cultivate Social and Emotional Skills

A number of educational organizations have developed training programs to help teachers work with kids in developing social and emotional skills. Kids for Change members are evaluating various programs to determine which program they would like to see implemented in their local schools. In this exercise, you will customize bullet and number formats, use navigation techniques that make it easy to quickly move around long documents, and format a large table to enhance its readability.

1. Open **W7-R2-SocLearningforKids** from your **Word Chapter 7** folder and save it as **W7-R2-SocLearningforKidsRevised**.
2. Scroll down and position the insertion point in the first bulleted list on page 1.
3. Choose **Home→Paragraph→Bullets** ▦ **menu button** ▾ and choose **Define New Bullet**.
4. Click the **Symbol** button.
5. Choose the **Webdings** font, scroll to the top of the gallery if necessary, choose the character shown (location may vary), and click **OK** twice.

6. Position the insertion point in the next bulleted list that starts at the bottom of page 1.
7. Choose **Home→Paragraph→Bullets menu button** ▾ and choose the same bullet, which appears in both the Recently Used Bullets and Document Bullets categories.
8. Use the same technique to change the bullets in the last bulleted list at the bottom of page 3.

   Now you will remove the new bullet so the next student who uses your computer will have the same experience.

9. Choose **Home→Paragraph→Bullets menu button** ▾.
10. Right-click the new bullet in the Bullet Library area and choose **Remove**.

Apply Numbers to a List

11. Scroll up and select the list that appears below the heading *The 12 Tools* at the top of page 3 and choose **Home→Paragraph→Numbering** ▦.

    Now you'll choose a different number format for the list.

12. Choose **Home→Paragraph→Numbering menu button** ▾ and then choose the format shown. (Location may vary.)

Notice that the last three numbers are left-aligned with the numbers above. They should be right-aligned.

13. Choose **Home→Paragraph→Numbering menu button** ▾ and then choose **Define New Number Format**.

14. Click the drop-down arrow in the Alignment field, choose **Right**, and then click **OK**.

    Notice how the numbers are now aligned.

Navigate in a Document

You know that you'll often have to navigate through this document as team members have questions about its contents, so you want to take some time to practice quick navigation techniques.

15. Press Ctrl+F to open the Navigation pane and type **toolbox** in the search field at the top of the Navigation pane.

16. Click the down-pointing arrow at the top of the Navigation pane several times to jump to the term.

17. Make sure the **Results** category at the top of the pane is active and then scroll down and click the last result in the list to jump to that location.

18. Click the **Headings** category at the top of the pane and click **Dovetail Learning** to jump to that location.

19. **Close** × the Navigation pane.

Insert a Bookmark

If there is a section of the document that you will return to frequently, using a bookmark provides a way to locate it easily.

20. Double-click *Dovetail* in the heading line.

21. Choose **Insert→Links→Bookmark** 🔖 and then type **Dovetail** in the Bookmark Name field and click **Add**.

22. Press Ctrl+Home or scroll up to move to the top of the document.

23. Choose **Insert→Links→Bookmark**.

24. Click **Go To** in the Bookmark dialog box to jump to the bookmark and then click **Close**.

Split the Window

Now you will compare the mission statements for Wings for Kids and Dovetail Learning.

25. Choose **View→Window→Split** ▢ and in the top window scroll to the top of page 1 until the mission statement is visible.

26. In the bottom window, scroll until the mission statement for Dovetail Learning is visible.

    This is an easy way to compare two different parts of a document.

27. Double-click the split bar in the middle of the window to return to one window.

28. Save and close the file.

Work with a Large Table

You will use the Members mailing list to send members the document about social learning. In preparation for that, you will now enhance the table by making it more readable.

29. Open **W7-R2-Members** and save it as **W7-R2-MembersRevised**.

30. Choose **Table Tools→Layout→Alignment→Cell Margins** ▣, change the top and bottom cell margins to **0.08**, and click **OK**.

   The table is now spilling over to the next page. You will repeat the header row so it will also appear at the top of the next page.

31. If necessary, position the insertion point in the header row of the table.

32. Choose **Table Tools→Layout→Cell Size→dialog box launcher** ⌐.

33. Click the **Row** tab, check the **Repeat as Header Row at the Top of Each Page**, and click **OK**.

34. Scroll down to see the header row at the top of the second page.

35. Save and close the file.

REINFORCE YOUR SKILLS: W7-R3

Format a Report on Childhood Obesity

Kids for Change is sponsoring a seminar on childhood obesity, presented by representatives from the World Health Organization and the Centers for Disease Control and Prevention. The organizations have already submitted background reading for the seminar. In this exercise, you will format the document to make the paragraphs and tables more engaging. You will also use techniques for navigating a long document.

1. Open **W7-R3-Obesity** from your **Word Chapter 7** folder and save it as **W7-R3-ObesityRevised**.

2. If the Styles task pane is not open, choose **Home→Styles→dialog box launcher** ⌐ to open it.

3. If necessary, position the insertion point in the heading at the top of the document and then choose the **Title** style from the task pane.

4. Scroll down to page 2, position the insertion point in the heading *CDC Introduction*, and apply the **Title** style.

5. Scroll back to the top of page 1 and position the insertion point in the first subtitle, which begins with *What can be done*.

6. Apply the **Subtitle** style from the Styles task pane and then apply **Subtitle** to the remaining headings:
   - General recommendations
   - Societal recommendations
   - What Needs to Be Done?
   - What Can Parents Do?

   You decide that the subtitles are not very appealing. Next, you will test a different theme to see if it improves the subtitles.

7. Choose **Design→Document Formatting→Themes** ▣ and choose **Parcel** from the gallery.

   Applying the Theme didn't really help the subtitles, so you will modify the Subtitle style.

8. Position the insertion point in the **first subtitle** at the top of page 1.

9. Hover the mouse pointer over **Subtitle** in the Styles task pane, click the drop-down arrow, and choose **Modify** from the menu.

10. In the Formatting area of the dialog box, click the **Italic** button and change the font size to **16 pt**, and then click **OK**.

11. Scroll through the document and notice that the subtitles updated throughout the document.

12. Scroll to the bottom of page 2 and notice the subtitle at the bottom of the page.

    It should be moved to the top of the next page.

13. Position the insertion point in front of the subtitle and press Ctrl + Enter to insert a page break and move the subtitle to the top of the next page.

14. Close the Styles task pane.

Customize Bullet Formats

15. Click the first item in the bulleted list on page 1, choose **Home→Paragraph→Bullets** ⊞ **menu button** ▾, and choose **Define New Bullet**.

16. Click the **Symbol** button in the Define New Bullet dialog box.

17. In the Symbol dialog box, choose the **Wingdings 2** font, scroll to about the middle of the list and choose the symbol shown, and then click **OK** twice.

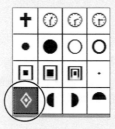

18. Scroll down to the next bulleted list and click in the first item.

19. Choose **Home→Paragraph→Bullets menu button** ▾ and choose the same button style from the Recently Used Bullets category.

20. Use the same technique to reformat the last bulleted list.

Navigate in a Long Document

21. Scroll to the top of page 2 and select *CDC* in the heading.

22. Choose **Insert→Links→Bookmark** 🔖.

23. Type **CDC** in the Bookmark Name field and click **Add**.

24. Press Ctrl + Home or scroll up to move to the top of the document.

25. Choose **Insert→Links→Bookmark**, click the **Go To** button to jump to the bookmark, and then close the dialog box.

26. Press Ctrl + F to open the Navigation pane and type **WHO** in the search field.

    The document scrolls to the first occurrence of WHO.

27. Click the insertion point in the page and then close the Navigation pane.

28. Choose **View→Window→Split** ⬜ and scroll in the bottom pane until the *CDC Introduction* heading appears.

    This is a great way to compare different parts of the same document without opening a separate window.

29. Double-click the split bar to return to a single window.

30. Save and close the file.

Work with a Long Table

Kids for Change has scheduled its programs and seminar topics well in advance, so it has plenty of time to coordinate the events. However, the table is not easy to read and to locate data. You will format the table to make it easier to work with.

31. Open **W7-R3-Programs** from your **Word Chapter 7** folder and save it as **W7-R3-ProgramsRevised**.

32. Position the insertion point in the table and choose **Table Tools→Layout→Alignment→Cell Margins** ▣.

33. Change the top and bottom margins to **0.08** and click **OK**.

    The increased margins caused the table to flow to the next page. Next, you will set up the header row to repeat on every page.

34. Position the insertion point in the header row at the top of the table.

35. Choose **Table Tools→Layout→Cell Size→dialog box launcher** ▫.

36. If necessary, click the **Row** tab, check **Repeat as Header Row at the Top of Each Page**, and then click **OK**.

37. Scroll to page 2 to see the repeating header row.

38. Save and close the file.

✎ Apply Your Skills

Multitask with Styles

Universal Corporate Events representatives, when planning a corporate event for a client, are often challenged with a juggling act of details ranging from hundreds of hotel reservations and travel accommodations to organizing meals and side trips. Your manager asked you to research the concept of multitasking and prepare a report on your findings. Your content has been approved, and it is now time to format the document to make it appealing to the reader. In this exercise, you will enhance the document by formatting with styles, themes, and style sets.

1. Open **W7-A1-Multitasking** from your **Word Chapter 7** folder and save it as **W7-A1-MultitaskingRevised**.

   You will start by creating a style by example.

2. Select the *Introduction* heading at the top of the document, apply the **Stencil** font, **16 pt**, and center the heading.

3. Open the Styles task pane and click the **New Style** button.

4. Follow these guidelines to complete the top part of the dialog box:
   - Name: **IntroStyle**
   - Style Type: **Paragraph**
   - Style Base On: **Normal**
   - Style for Following Paragraph: **Normal**

5. If necessary, check the **Add to the Styles Gallery** checkbox at the bottom of the dialog box and click **OK**.

   Notice that the new style appears in the Styles gallery on the Ribbon and in the Styles task pane. Next, you will apply a built-in style and then modify it.

6. Position the insertion point in the next heading, *The multitasking myth*, and then apply the **Heading 2** style.

7. Hover the mouse pointer over the **Heading 2** style in the Styles task pane, click the drop-down arrow, and choose **Modify**.

8. Click the **Format** button at the bottom of the dialog box and choose **Font**.

9. In the Font dialog box, set the font to **Bold**, **14 pt**, and the color **Black**, **Text 1**.

10. Check the **Small Caps** checkbox and then click **OK** twice.

11. Apply the modified **Heading 2** style to the rest of the subtitles in the document:
    - You're not really multitasking
    - It's slowing you down
    - You're making mistakes
    - You're not actually good at it

    Next, you will work with themes and style sets to enhance your formatting.

12. Choose **Design→Document Formatting→Themes** and choose **Parallax**.

13. Choose **Design**→**Document Formatting** and then click the **More** button and apply the **Shaded** style set.

    Next, you will modify the theme color.

14. Choose **Design**→**Document Formatting**→**Colors** and choose **Paper**.

    You've decided to change the Introduction *heading to make it blend better with the subheadings.*

15. Position the insertion point in the *Introduction* heading and choose the **Title** style from the Styles task pane.

16. You don't plan to use the IntroStyle anymore, so using the Styles task pane, delete the style and then close the task pane.

17. Click the **Home** tab and notice that the IntroStyle has been removed from the Styles gallery on the Ribbon.

    There is a heading at the bottom of page 1 that should be moved to the top of page 2.

18. Position the insertion point in front of the heading at the bottom of page 1 and press Ctrl + Enter to move it to the top of page 2.

19. Save and close the file.

APPLY YOUR SKILLS: W7-A2

Plan a Bicycle Trip in the Loire Valley

A client of Universal Corporate Events is planning a bicycling trip in the Loire Valley of France as a reward for Employee of the Year winners in each of its branch offices. Universal Corporate Events is providing a sample itinerary for the client to review. In this exercise, you will polish the sample itinerary for the trip. And the client has requested a list of châteaux in the Loire Valley, so you will prepare that in a table and format it for ease of reading.

1. Open **W7-A2-LoireTour** from your **Word Chapter 7** folder and save it as **W7-A2-LoireTourRevised**.

2. Position the insertion point in the first bulleted item.

3. Define a new bullet that uses the Wingdings 3 symbol shown here.

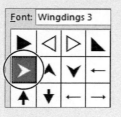

    Now you'll apply the new bullet to the remaining bulleted items.

4. Position the insertion point in the next bulleted item and choose **Home**→**Paragraph**→ **Bullets menu button** ▾.

    The new bullet appears in the Recently Used Bullets category.

5. Click the bullet, scroll through the document, and notice that the bullet was applied to the rest of the bulleted items.

    Next, you will use nonbreaking spaces to keep a name together on a line.

6. Scroll to the second-to-last line in the *Day 3* paragraph, position the insertion point after *Leonardo* and delete the space.

7. Choose **Insert→Symbols→Symbol** and choose **More Symbols**.

8. Choose **Nonbreaking Space** in the Special Characters tab and then finish inserting the character.

   Remember the keystrokes for a nonbreaking space: [Ctrl]+[Shift]+[Space].

9. Position the insertion point after *da*, delete the space, and then press [Ctrl]+[Shift]+[Space] to insert another nonbreaking space.

10. If necessary, display formatting marks and notice the symbol used for nonbreaking spaces.

Navigate in a Long Document

Next, you will insert a bookmark for navigating in the document.

11. Create a bookmark for the text *Day 6*, using **Day6** as the bookmark name.

12. Move to the top of the document and then use the Bookmark feature to jump to Day 6.

    Now you will locate a term in the document.

13. Open the Navigation pane, type **Day 1** in the search field, and then position the insertion point in the **Day 1** page.

14. Click the **Headings** button at the top of the Navigation pane, click the **Day 4** heading to jump to that location, and then close the **Navigation** pane.

    Next you will split the window so you can compare different parts of the document.

15. Choose **View→Window→Split** and then scroll the top window to **Day 1** and the bottom window to **Day 6**.

16. Double-click the split bar to return to one window.

17. Save and close the file.

Work with a Large Table

You will make some modifications to a table to improve its readability. You'll begin by increasing the cell margins and then repeat the header row for each page.

18. Open **W7-A2-Chateaux** from your **Word Chapter 7** folder and save it as **W7-A2-ChateauxRevised**.

19. Position the insertion point in the table, choose **Table Tools→Layout→Alignment→ Cell Margins**, and change the top and bottom margins to **0.08**.

20. With the insertion point in the first row of the table, choose **Table Tools→Layout→ Cell Size dialog box launcher**.

21. Use the **Row** tab in the Table Properties dialog box to repeat the header row on each page.

22. Scroll to the top of page 2 to see the repeated header row.

23. Save and close the file.

Prepare Cuban Travel Information for a Client

Universal Corporate Events has asked you to research information about travel to Cuba, and your research has been approved. In this exercise, you will format the document so it can be presented to clients.

1. Open **W7-A3-CubaTravel** from your **Word Chapter 7** folder and save it as **W7-A3-CubaTravelRevised**.

2. Apply the **Heading 1** style to the *Cuba Background* heading at the top of the document.

   Hint: If necessary, display the Styles task pane.

3. Apply the **Heading 2** style to the headings *U.S.–Cuba Relations*, *U.S. Assistance to Cuba*, and *Bilateral Economic Relations*.

4. Scroll down to the *Outdoor Activity* heading and apply the **Heading 1** style.

5. Scroll down to the *Top-Rated Cuban Tourist Attractions* heading and apply the **Heading 1** style.

   Next you will modify the theme and style set.

6. Apply the **Metropolitan** theme to the document and then open the Style Sets gallery and choose **Basic (Simple)**.

   Next, you will modify the heading styles.

7. Position the insertion point in the *Cuba Background* heading and then modify the **Heading 1** style by changing the font color to **Brown, Accent 3**.

8. Scroll to page 3 and notice that the other Heading 1 styles were updated.

9. Position the insertion point in the *U.S.-Cuba Relations* heading and then modify the **Heading 2** style to use the font color **Brown, Accent 3**.

10. Close the **Styles** task pane then scroll down to see that the other Heading 2 headings updated.

11. Scroll to page 3, position the insertion point in the first bulleted item, and define a new bullet using the symbol character shown from the **Wingdings** font.

Format a Table for Readability

12. Scroll to the table and change the top and bottom cell margins to **0.08**.

13. Repeat the header row on all pages.

    Now you will add a caption to the table.

14. Scroll to the bottom of the table and position the insertion point on the first blank line below the table.

15. Insert **Excerpt from PlanetWare Website** as the table caption.

    Notice the number 1 appears at the end of the caption. Because there is only one table in the document, the number is not necessary.

16. Delete the number **1** at the end of the caption.

17. Save and close the file; exit Word.

◢ Extend Your Skills

These exercises challenge you to think critically and apply your new skills. You will be evaluated on your ability to follow directions, completeness, creativity, and the use of proper grammar and mechanics. Save files to your chapter folder. Submit assignments as directed.

W7-E1   That's the Way I See It

You have just started your own personal training business and will advertise your business with an informative brochure (maximum two pages) to be distributed through local businesses in the community. Decide on a name for your business. Include a mission statement and a description of your background qualifications. Create a bulleted list of the services you offer and another bulleted list of the benefits your clients will enjoy. Customize the bullets using a symbol of your choice. Use Word's built-in heading styles to make your brochure professional-looking and easy to read. Customize the headings using themes and style sets and any other modifications you wish to make. Create a table listing classes you offer, short descriptions of the classes, and the days and times the classes will meet. Apply the table style of your choice and increase the cell margins to add white space. Don't forget your contact information. Feel free to use an Internet search to gather ideas to assist you with content. Save your file as **W7-E1-Exercise**.

W7-E2   Be Your Own Boss

You want to increase your customer base at Blue Jean Landscaping, so you will create a one- or two-page flyer advertising your business. Write an "About Us" paragraph describing the services you offer and include a mission statement. Also, write a paragraph or two about your background qualifications. Include another paragraph about the pesticide safety techniques you employ at your company. Blue Jean Landscaping saves customers money by having them provide the labor for their projects. Create a bulleted list of the physical tasks customers will accomplish to take advantage of your cost-cutting offer. Create a table listing classes you offer, such as "How to Plant Roses," to educate your customers in the skills they need to provide the labor for their gardens. Use built-in heading styles to section off the different parts of the flyer and modify the styles to suit your taste. Customize the bullets for your bulleted list, format the table with a table style, and add white space to the table by increasing cell margins. If necessary, search the Internet for information about landscaping companies to help you with the content. Save the file as **W7-E2-Landscape**.

W7-E3   Demonstrate Proficiency

As the owner of Stormy BBQ, you are proud of serving only locally grown, organic vegetables and free-range, farm-raised pork and beef. Create a two-page flyer to distribute to customers at the cash register. Include a mission statement and a paragraph or two describing the history of Stormy BBQ and include one or two customer testimonials. Create a bulleted list of the benefits of eating locally produced food. Insert a menu in the form of a table that spans two pages and add a caption to the table. Use custom styles that you create from scratch to section off the topics in your flyer and create custom bullets for your list. Apply a table style to your menu, add white space for ease of reading, and repeat the header row at the top of page 2. Conduct an Internet search if you need help with the menu or benefits of the healthy food you serve. Save the file as **W7-E3-BBQ.**

8 | Organizing Long Documents

Plowing through a long document can be challenging for the reader if it is not well-organized. Word offers several great tools for organizing documents. A table of contents and an index help readers locate specific topics and terms. Headers and footers display important information, such as page numbers and chapter names. In this chapter, you will work with these tools, organizing long documents and making them more accessible to the reader.

LEARNING OBJECTIVES

▸ Create a table of contents

▸ Work with multiple headers and footers

▸ Insert an index

▸ Keep text together

▸ Add a watermark

⊳ Project: Organizing a Long Document

The Raritan Clinic East policies and procedures manual contains principles and guidelines adopted by the clinic to reach its long-term goals. It influences all major decisions and activities in day-to-day operations. You recently accepted a position in the human resources department at Raritan Clinic. You have been tasked with reviewing the current policies and procedures manual, and you have identified numerous "finishing" features that need to be added to the manual to make it easier to use. By adding a table of contents, index, and headers and footers, you believe the document will be more user-friendly.

Creating a Table of Contents

Readers appreciate a good table of contents. It outlines the document and adds a professional appearance. And if the document is electronic, the table of contents links provide Internet-like navigation.

The Table of Contents (TOC) feature automatically builds a table of contents by gathering up the headings that are formatted with heading styles. The headings in the TOC are organized in the sequence in which they appear in the document. In addition, TOC styles are applied that correspond to the heading levels. The styles then format the table entries. For example, Heading 2 entries are subordinate to Heading 1 entries. You can automatically update a table of contents created with the built-in heading styles.

You can apply a predesigned table of contents format from the Table of Contents gallery, or you can create a custom table of contents, which gives you more control over the formatting.

≡ References→Table of Contents→Table of Contents 📄

Creating a Page for the Table of Contents

In most documents, the table of contents appears either at the beginning of the document or just after the title page in documents containing a title page. Because the table of contents is often created after the document is complete, you may need to create a new page to hold the table.

When headers and footers or other page-level formatting such as page numbering appears in a document, it is better to create a page to hold the table of contents using a section break. This allows flexibility, such as numbering the table of contents page(s) with Roman numerals (i, ii, iii) and the rest of the document with Arabic numerals (1, 2, 3).

Table of Contents Links

A table of contents is inserted as a large field composed of various table entries. Each entry within the table functions as a hyperlink. You can quickly navigate in the document using the links.

> **Table of Contents**
>
> Mission Statement ....
>
> Scope of Services ┌──────────────────────┐ ....
>   │ Current Document   │
>   │ Ctrl+Click to follow link │
>   └──────────────────────┘
>
> Patient Management Procedures ....

DEVELOP YOUR SKILLS: W8-D1

In this exercise, you will open the Raritan Clinic East policies and procedures manual and review its heading styles. Then you will create a table of contents and navigate in the document using the links. Finally, you will remove the table of contents.

1. Start Word, open **W8-D1-RaritanP&P** from your **Word Chapter 8** folder, and save it as **W8-D1-RaritanP&PRevised**.

2. Choose **Home→Styles→dialog box launcher** ⌐.

3. Scroll to the first page of the body of the document and position the insertion point in the heading *Mission Statement*.

   Notice that Heading 1 in the Styles task pane is highlighted, indicating that it is the style used to format the heading.

4. Position the insertion point in several additional headings on page 2.

   You will notice that both Heading 1 and Heading 2 styles are on the page.

5. Close the Styles task pane and then position the insertion point in front of the heading *Mission Statement*.

   Now you will insert a section break to create a blank page for the table of contents.

6. Choose **Layout→Page Setup→Breaks** ⊟ and then choose **Next Page**.

7. If necessary, display formatting marks; then scroll up and position the insertion point to the right of the paragraph symbol, just in front of the section break, and tap ⸢Enter⸥.

8. Choose **References→Table of Contents→Table of Contents** 📄 and then choose **Automatic Table 2** from the gallery.

9. Scroll up and review the table of contents.

   You can see that the headings in the document are used as the table of contents entries.

Navigate Using Hyperlinks

10. Hover the mouse pointer over the *Initial Diagnostic Evaluation* entry in the table and notice the pop-up message.

11. Press ⸢Ctrl⸥ and click the link, and Word jumps to that heading in the document.

12. Scroll up to the top of the table of contents and then click the table to select it.

13. Click the **Table of Contents** 📄 button in the upper-left corner and choose **Remove Table of Contents** at the bottom of the menu.

14. Save the file.

The Update Table Button

When you make changes to headings or move text in a document, you need to update the table of contents. There is an Update Table button that makes this task easy. Whenever the insertion point is anywhere in the table of contents, two buttons appear in the upper-left corner of the table.

The Table of Contents button displays the Table of Contents gallery, including a command to remove the table.

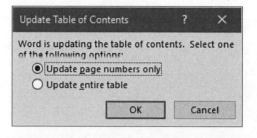

The Update Table button updates the table of contents with the latest changes.

When you click the Update Table button, a dialog box presents options for updating page numbers only or the entire table. Choose the page numbers option if you have been adding text but haven't changed any headings.

 You can right-click a table of contents and choose Update Field from the menu.

≡ References→Table of Contents→Update Table | F9

The Table of Contents Dialog Box

The Table of Contents gallery provides the fastest method for creating a table of contents, but if you wish to have more control over the formatting of your table, you can use the Table of Contents dialog box. When you use the dialog box, you must also manually add the title that precedes the table. In addition, there are no Table of Contents or Update Table buttons at the top of the table as there are for a table generated from the Table of Contents gallery. To update a manual table of contents, you can use the F9 shortcut keystroke.

View the video "Creating a Custom Table of Contents."

DEVELOP YOUR SKILLS: W8-D2

In this exercise, you will insert a custom table of contents using the Table of Contents dialog box. Then you will edit a heading and update the table of contents.

1. Save your file as **W8-D2-RaritanP&PRevised** and, if necessary, display formatting marks.

   The insertion point should be just to the left of the section break at the top of the blank table of contents page.

2. Tap Enter to create a new, blank line.

   The blank line will hold the title. Next you will reformat its paragraph symbol with your desired title formatting.

3. Follow these steps to format and add the table title:

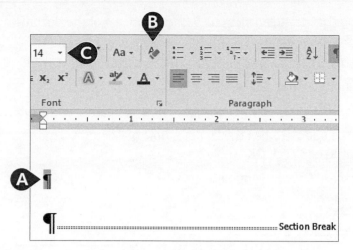

- Ⓐ Select this paragraph symbol.
- Ⓑ Choose **Home→Font→Clear All Formatting**.
- Ⓒ Change the font size to **14 pt**.

4. Type **Table of Contents** and tap Enter.

5. Choose **References→Table of Contents→Table of Contents** 📄.

6. Choose **Custom Table of Contents** at the bottom of the gallery to open the Table of Contents dialog box.

7. Follow these steps to generate a table of contents:

- Ⓐ Make sure these checkboxes are checked.
- Ⓑ Make sure that dots are chosen here.
- Ⓒ Choose **Formal** as the format.
- Ⓓ Click **OK**.

8. Scroll to the bottom of the table and delete the extra paragraph symbol.

WORD

Edit a Heading and Update the Table of Contents

9. Locate the heading *Patient Attendance and Billing* on page 4 of the document and change *Attendance* to **Appointments**.

Now that you have made a change in a heading, you need to update the table of contents.

10. Scroll up and position the insertion point in the table of contents.

Notice that there is no Update Table button in the upper-left corner of the table.

11. Tap F9 to begin the update; when the Update Table of Contents dialog box appears, choose **Update Entire Table** and click **OK**.

The word Attendance *changed to* Appointments.

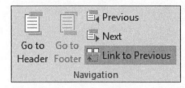

12. Save your file.

Multiple Headers and Footers

Initially, the header and footer content is the same throughout a document because the Link to Previous feature is turned on by default, as shown in this illustration.

When a document contains multiple sections, you can break the link between sections and thereby create a new header and footer for each document section. For example, suppose you want to number the front portion of a long document using small Roman numerals and the body of the document using Arabic numerals. Separating the document into sections is the first important step before creating multiple headers and footers within a document.

Restarting and Formatting Page Numbers

When you have more than one section in a document, you may wish to control the starting page number within a section. Typically, the body of a document should start at page 1 rather than continuing the Roman numerals from the front matter. You may also want to control the page number formats. The Page Number Format dialog box provides options to restart numbering and to modify the number format, such as changing from Roman numerals to Arabic numerals.

You can choose from a variety of page numbering formats.

You can continue page numbering from the previous section or restart numbering with a specific number.

Different First Page Header or Footer

There may be times when all you want to do is set up a different header or footer on the first page of a document. For example, suppose you want all pages of a document numbered in the footer area of each page except for the cover page. You can set a different first page header or footer simply by choosing the Different First Page option.

DEVELOP YOUR SKILLS: W8-D3

In this exercise, you will insert header text that will appear in both sections of the document. You will also break the connection between footers so you can have different footers in each section, and then you will change the starting page number on the second page of the document.

1. Save your file as **W8-D3-RaritanP&PRevised** and, if necessary, display formatting characters.
2. Position the insertion point in **section 2**, which begins with *Mission Statement*.
3. Choose **Insert→Header & Footer→Header** ☐ and then choose **Edit Header** at the bottom of the gallery.

4. Take a moment to observe the header area.

┌───┐
│   │
│   ¶   │
│ ┌──────────────┐ - - - - - - - - - - - - - - - - - - - ┌────────────┐ │
│ │Header -Section 2-│ Mission·Statement¶   │Same as Previous│ │
└───┘

The Header -Section 2- tab indicates that the insertion point is in the header area of section 2; the Same as Previous tab indicates that text you type in section 2 will carry over to the previous section. In other words, the sections are linked. You want the header sections to be linked in this instance because the word DRAFT should appear on all pages. You'll add that next.

5. Tap ⟨Tab⟩ to position the insertion point at the center of the header area and then type **DRAFT**.

6. Format the header text with **bold**, **14 pt**, and then double-click in the body of the document to close the header area.

7. Scroll up to the table of contents.

Notice that the word DRAFT appears in the header. That's because the headers in both sections are linked. Now you will add a footer that appears in only one section.

8. Scroll down and position the insertion point in **section 2**.

9. Choose **Insert→Header & Footer→Footer** 🗋 and then choose **Edit Footer**.

Notice the Same as Previous tab in the footer area. You don't want the footer text to appear on the table of contents page, so you will break the link.

10. Choose **Header & Footer Tools→Design→Navigation**.

The Link to Previous button is highlighted, meaning it is turned on and the footers in sections 1 and 2 are linked.

11. Click the **Link to Previous** 🔳 button to turn it off and break the link between the two sections.

The Same as Previous tab at the right side of the footer area disappeared.

12. Choose **Header & Footer Tools→Design→Header & Footer→Footer** 🗋 and then choose **Blank**.

13. Click **Type Here** and type **Policies & Procedures Manual**.

14. Tap ⟨Tab⟩ to position the insertion point in the center of the footer area and then type **Raritan Clinic East**.

15. Tap ⟨Tab⟩ to position the insertion point at the right side of the footer.

16. Choose **Header & Footer Tools→Design→Header & Footer→Page Number** 🔲.

17. Choose **Current Position** and then choose **Plain Number**.

Change the Starting Page Number

You want to start numbering with a 1 on the first page of the document body.

18. Choose **Header & Footer Tools→Design→Header & Footer→Page Number** 🔲.

19. Choose **Format Page Numbers** and then choose **Start At**.

    Number 1 is chosen automatically, but you could change it if you needed to.

20. Click **OK** to restart page numbering with a 1 and then double-click in the document body to close the header and footer areas.

21. Scroll up and notice that the footer does not appear on the table of contents page.

22. Scroll down and observe the footer text in the rest of the document.

    Because the page numbering changed, you need to update the table of contents again.

23. Scroll to the table of contents and position the insertion point in the table of contents.

24. Tap ⌨F9, choose **Update Entire Table**, and then click **OK**.

25. Save your file.

Creating an Index

Adding an index to a document gives the reader an easy way to find important words. To create an index, you mark the entries and then generate the index. The entries you mark are sorted alphabetically and their page numbers are inserted.

Marking Index Entries

When entries and subentries are marked, it's important to note that marking index entries is a case-sensitive action. If you mark all occurrences of a word such as *Billing* for inclusion in the index, only those occurrences of the word where the *B* is capitalized are marked. So, it's important to consider which occurrences you want marked before selecting Mark All.

⚠ View the video "Main Entries and Subentries."

☰ References→Index→Mark Entry

☰ References→Index→Insert Index

☰ References→Index→Update Index

DEVELOP YOUR SKILLS: W8-D4

In this exercise, you will mark index entries and subentries in preparation for generating an index.

1. Save your file as **W8-D4-RaritanP&PRevised**.

2. Go to the first page of the body of the manual and select the heading *Mission Statement*.

3. Choose **References→Index→Mark Entry** 🔲.

   Now you will edit the main entry text.

4. Type **Goals** in the Main Entry field to replace the text that was automatically inserted in the Mark Index Entry dialog box.

   The text that was in the field came from the words you selected in the document. You can always replace or edit the suggested entries in this manner.

5. Click **Mark** at the bottom of the dialog box.

   Now you will examine an index code.

6. If necessary, drag the dialog box to the side and notice that the code { XE "Goals" } was inserted into the document.

   This code identifies Goals as a main index entry.

7. Select the word *specialties* at the end of the second line in the second paragraph under the *Mission Statement* heading.

8. Click the Mark Index Entry dialog box to activate it and then click **Mark** to use the proposed text as the main entry.

9. Select *General Medicine* in the first line of the third paragraph below Scope of Services, click the dialog box to activate it, and click **Mark**.

10. Scroll down and select *Patient* in the heading *Patient Appointments and Billing,* click the dialog box, and click **Mark**.

Mark All Entries

Depending on the nature of the document you are marking, there may be text you want to mark every time it appears.

11. Select *Billing* in the heading *Patient Appointments and Billing* and then click the dialog box.

12. Click **Mark All** to mark all occurrences of *Billing* for inclusion in the index.

    *Remember, it only marks **Billing** if it begins with a capital letter.*

13. Select *billing* toward the end of the first line in the third paragraph below *Patient Appointments and Billing,* click the dialog box, and click **Mark All**.

Mark Subentries

14. If necessary, scroll down to the *Patient Records* heading; then follow these steps to mark records as a subentry:

   Ⓐ Select *Patient* in the heading.

   Ⓑ Click the **Mark Index Entry** dialog box to activate it.

   Ⓒ Type `records` in the Subentry field and click **Mark**.

15. Navigate to the second paragraph below the *Patient Records* heading, select *files* in the first line, and click the dialog box to activate it.

16. Double-click *files* in the Main Entry field and then press Ctrl+X.

17. Click the **Subentry** field and then press Ctrl+V to paste *files* into the field.

18. Type `Patient` in the Main Entry field and then click **Mark**.

19. Close the **Mark Index Entry** dialog box.

20. Save your file.

Generating Index Entries Using a Concordance

If a document is extremely long, marking index entries can be overwhelming. There is an automatic option for marking words and phrases to be included in an index. This option allows you to create a list of words and phrases you want to include and saves it as a separate file that acts as a concordance file.

When you use a concordance file to generate an index, it's important to know how it works. These guidelines will provide you with some basic information.

▸ The list of words and phrases to be included as main entries should be typed in one column straight down the left margin of the document or in the first column of a table.

▸ The document should contain only the words and phrases to be marked.

▸ To mark entries with subentries, create the concordance using a table layout. In the first column, type the words you want to mark as the main entry. In the second column, type the main entry followed by a colon, followed by the text for the subentry, without spaces.

patient	patient:records

▸ Entries can be listed in any order in the concordance. They will be sorted and grouped alphabetically when you generate the index. However, sorting the words helps identify duplicate words in the concordance.

DEVELOP YOUR SKILLS: W8-D5

In this exercise, you will mark index entries using a concordance document.

1. Save your file as **W8-D5-RaritanP&PRevised**.
2. Open **W8-D5-P&PConcordance** from your **Word Chapter 8** folder.
3. Scroll through the document, review its contents, and then close the document.
4. Position the insertion point anywhere on the title page at the top of the document.
5. Choose **References→Index→Insert Index** 📄.
6. Click **AutoMark** at the bottom of the dialog box to display the Open Index AutoMark File dialog box.
7. Navigate to your **Word Chapter 8** folder and double-click **W8-D5-P&PConcordance**.

   Although nothing appears to happen, the list of words and phrases in the concordance is compared with the manual. When a word is located, the entry is automatically marked in the manual.

8. Scroll through and review the document.

   Notice the numerous index marks that were added from the concordance in addition to the individual marked items from the previous exercise.

9. Turn off formatting marks.

   Because index codes can be quite lengthy, displaying them can cause text to roll onto other pages. Turning off formatting marks ensures that page numbers are accurate.

10. Save the file.

Inserting and Updating the Index

After all the index entries are marked, you can insert the index using the Index dialog box. You can choose the overall format for the index and select several other formatting options. You can update an index in the same manner as a table of contents.

≡ References→Table of Contents→Update Index | F9

There are several ways you can modify an index once you create it. You can:

▶ use the Index dialog box to change various formatting options.

▶ format the index directly.

▶ change the text of an entry by replacing it directly in the code that was originally created and then update the index.

▶ delete an entry by removing the code and updating the index.

Note! *The format that's active in the Index dialog box will be reapplied if you update the index.*

DEVELOP YOUR SKILLS: W8-D6

In this exercise, you will generate and format an index.

1. Save your file as **W8-D6-RaritanP&PRevised**.
2. Press Ctrl + End or scroll down to move to the end of the document.

   An index should begin on a blank page.
3. Type the heading **Index** and tap Enter.
4. Select the heading and format the text as **bold, 16 pt**.
5. Position the insertion point on the blank line below the Index heading.
6. Choose **References→Index→Insert Index** 📄.
7. Choose **Formal** from the Formats list at the bottom of the dialog box and then click **OK**.

Modify the Index Format

8. Click anywhere in the index and then choose **References→Index→Insert Index** 📄.
9. Choose **Modern** at the bottom of the dialog box and then choose **Run-In** at the top-right corner.
10. Click **OK**; click **OK** again when the message appears asking if you want to replace the index.

    The new index is inserted with the Run-In number style. Notice how the style affects the subentries. You've decided you like the previous indented subentries.
11. Click **Undo** ↩ to reverse the change.
12. Save the file.

Keeping Text Together

If you're working on a long document that goes through multiple revision cycles, controlling pagination can be a challenge. There are several options in the Paragraph dialog box that can be helpful.

> **Paragraph**
>
> Indents and Spacing | Line and Page Breaks
>
> **Pagination**
> - ☑ Widow/Orphan control
> - ☐ Keep with next
> - ☐ Keep lines together
> - ☐ Page break before

- **Widow/Orphan Control:** Places at least two lines of a paragraph at the top or bottom of a page; checked by default

- **Keep with Next:** Forces a paragraph to appear with the paragraph that follows it; often used to keep a heading with the following paragraph

- **Keep Lines Together:** Prevents a page break in the middle of a paragraph

- **Page Break Before:** Forces a page break before a specific paragraph

DEVELOP YOUR SKILLS: W8-D7

In this exercise, you will use the Keep with Next option to ensure that specified segments of text stay together when a document is automatically paginated.

1. Save your file as **W8-D7-RaritanP&PRevised**.

2. On the first page of the document body, select the *Patient Management Procedures* heading and the *Entry into Services* subheading.

   A heading should not appear alone at the page bottom. Although that is not the case now, further editing may split a heading from the paragraph that follows.

3. Choose **Home→Paragraph→dialog box launcher** ⊡.

4. If necessary, click the **Line and Page Breaks** tab, check **Keep with Next**, and click **OK**.

   This ensures that the heading, the subheading, and the paragraph following the subheading will "stick together" during future edits and automatic pagination.

5. Scroll down to the next page and select the *Patient Appointments and Billing* heading.

6. Choose **Home→Paragraph→dialog box launcher** ⊡, check **Keep with Next**, and click **OK**.

7. Save your file.

Watermarks

A watermark is text or a graphic placed behind text or other objects in a document; it is visible only in Print Layout or Read Mode view. Some common watermarks include a faint image of the word *Draft* or *Confidential* in the background.

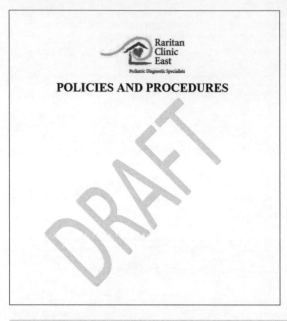

≡ Design→Page Background→Watermark

DEVELOP YOUR SKILLS: W8-D8

The changes made to the policies and procedures manual need to be approved by your manager. Although the word DRAFT appears in the header, you've decided that using the word as a watermark would be more effective. In this exercise, you will delete the term in the header and then add a watermark to the document.

1. Save your file as **W8-D8-RaritanP&PRevised**.
2. Position the insertion point at the top of the document and double-click the header area to open it.
3. Select the word *DRAFT* and tap Delete.
4. Double-click in the body of the document to close the header area.
5. Choose **Design→Page Background→Watermark** and then choose **Draft 1** from the gallery.
6. Scroll through a few pages to view the watermark.
7. Save and close the file; exit Word.

Self-Assessment

 Check your knowledge of this chapter's key concepts and skills using the Self-Assessment in your ebook or eLab course.

Reinforce Your Skills

Organize a Document with a TOC and Headers and Footers

Kids for Change is providing background reading for its next monthly meeting in which it'll brainstorm new ideas to help kids in the community thrive. You will add a table of contents and headers and footers to make the document more accessible to the readers.

1. Start Word, open **W8-R1-Organizations** from your **Word Chapter 8** folder, and save it as **W8-R1-OrganizationsRevised**.

2. If necessary, display formatting marks; then choose **Home→Styles→dialog box launcher** ⌐ to open the Styles task pane.

3. Starting on the first page of the main body of the document, position the insertion point in the headings and notice the heading styles in effect.

4. Close the Styles task pane.

5. On page 2, notice the section break at the top of the page.

6. Position the insertion point on the blank line above the section break.

7. Choose **References→Table of Contents→Table of Contents** 📄 and then choose **Automatic Table 1** from the gallery.

Modify a Heading

8. Scroll to page 3 and, in the first subheading below *Change for Kids*, select *Tutoring* and replace it with **Teaching**.

9. On page 2, position the insertion point in the table of contents and click **Update Table** 📄 at the top of the table of contents border.

10. Choose **Update Entire Table** and click **OK**.

Create a Custom Table of Contents

11. Choose **References→Table of Contents→Table of Contents** and then choose **Custom Table of Contents**.

12. Make sure all three checkboxes are checked and then, if necessary, choose **Formal** from the Formats drop-down list.

```
☑ Show page numbers              ☑ Use hyperlinks instead of page numbers
☑ Right align page numbers
Tab leader:  ........   ⌄

General
Formats:   Formal              ⌄
Show levels:  3   ⬍
```

13. Click **OK**; when the message appears confirming the replacement, click **OK** again.

Add Multiple Headers and Footers

14. Position the insertion point in section 2 of the document, which begins with *Introduction*.

15. Choose **Insert→Header & Footer→Header** 🗎 and then choose **Edit Header**.

    Notice the Same as Previous tab at the right side of the header area. You will now break the link between sections 1 and 2.

16. Choose **Header & Footer Tools→Design→Navigation→Link to Previous** 🔲.

    Notice that the Same as Previous tab no longer appears at the right side of the header.

17. Tap ⌷Tab⌷ to position the insertion point in the center of the header and then type **Kids for Change**.

18. Double-click in the body of the document to close the header area.

19. Scroll up and notice that the header doesn't appear on pages 1 and 2; scroll down and observe the header on pages 3 and 4.

20. If necessary, position the insertion point in the page starting with *Introduction*, which is section 2.

21. Choose **Insert→Header & Footer→Footer** 🗎 and then choose **Edit Footer**.

    Notice the Same as Previous tab at the right side of the footer area.

22. Choose **Header & Footer Tools→Design→Navigation→Link to Previous** to break the link between sections 1 and 2.

23. Choose **Header & Footer Tools→Design→Header & Footer→Footer** and then choose **Austin**.

    Notice that the Austin format placed a border around the page and that page numbering starts at page 2. You will now change the numbering to start on page 1.

24. Choose **Header & Footer Tools→Design→Header & Footer→Page Number** 🔲 and then choose **Format Page Numbers**.

25. In the Page Number Format dialog box, choose **Start At** from the bottom of the dialog box.

    The number defaults to 1, which is what you want.

26. Click **OK** and then double-click in the body of the document to close the footer area.

27. Scroll down and notice the numbering on the third and fourth pages; scroll up and notice that there are no footers on the first two pages.

28. Save and close the file.

REINFORCE YOUR SKILLS: W8-R2

Add an Index to a Document

The leader for the next Kids for Change monthly meeting is providing members with a document containing ideas for how kids can promote sustainability, which is the topic of the meeting. In this exercise, you will create an index for the document so members can easily locate important terms.

1. Open **W8-R2-Sustainability** from your **Word Chapter 8** folder and save it as **W8-R2-SustainabilityRevised**.

2. If necessary, display formatting marks; then select *wood products* in the first bullet point.

3. Choose **References→Index→Mark Entry** 🗎.

    That places wood products in the Main Entry field.

4. Type **salvaged** in the Subentry field and then click **Mark**.

*Notice the colon between **wood products** and **salvaged** in the index code in the document. This indicates that **salvaged** is a subentry of **wood products**.*

5. Select *salvaged* in the Subentry field, type **recycled** in its place, and click **Mark**.

This adds another subentry for wood products.

6. Select *light bulbs* in the third bullet point and then click the dialog box to activate it.

7. Type **fluorescent** in the Subentry field and then click **Mark**.

8. Now change the subentry text to **standard** and click **Mark**.

This adds another subentry for light bulbs.

9. Select *paper products* in the fifth bullet point, click the dialog box, and click **Mark**.

10. Select *recycle* in the second line of the sixth bullet point and then click the dialog box.

11. Mark the following terms as subentries for *recycle*.
    - wood products
    - paper products
    - plastic containers
    - cell phones
    - electronics

12. Close the dialog box.

Insert an Index

13. Press $\boxed{\text{Ctrl}}$+$\boxed{\text{End}}$ or scroll down to move to the end of the document and then press $\boxed{\text{Ctrl}}$+$\boxed{\text{Enter}}$ to insert a page break.

14. Type **Index** and tap $\boxed{\text{Enter}}$, format the heading with **bold**, **16 pt**, and then position the insertion point on the blank line below the heading.

15. Turn off formatting marks.

Remember, displaying index codes can affect page numbering.

16. Choose **References→Index→Insert Index** 📄.

17. Follow these guidelines to complete the index:
    - Choose **Classic** in the Formats list.
    - Check the **Right Align Page Numbers** checkbox.
    - Choose **dots** in the Tab Leader field.

☑ Right align page numbers	
Ta**b** leader:	.... ⌄
Forma**t**s:	Classic ⌄

18. Click **OK**.

Modify an Entry and Update the Index

19. Scroll to the second-to-last bullet point and select *Computer Takeback Campaign*.

20. Choose **References→Index→Mark Entry**.

This phrase will be a subentry under recycle, so you will cut the term and paste it into the Subentry field.

21. Press `Ctrl`+`X`, position the insertion point in the **Subentry** field, and press `Ctrl`+`V`.

22. Type `recycle` in the Main Entry field and then click **Mark**.

23. Close the dialog box and scroll down to the index.

24. Turn off formatting marks.

   Formatting marks were turned on when you marked the last entry.

25. Hover the mouse pointer over the index, right-click, and choose **Update Field**.

Finalize the Document

This document will go through some revisions, so you want to be sure the lines in the second-to-last bullet point don't split between pages if repagination takes place.

26. Scroll up and select the bullet point that begins with *Recycle old electronics*.

27. Choose **Home→Paragraph→dialog box launcher** `⌐`.

28. If necessary, click the **Line and Page Breaks** tab, check **Keep Lines Together**, and click **OK**.

   Now you will insert a DRAFT watermark so this document isn't mistaken for the final version.

29. Choose **Design→Page Background→Watermark** and choose **Draft 2** from the gallery.

30. Save and close the file.

REINFORCE YOUR SKILLS: W8-R3

Organize a Long Document

Kids for Change is planning a fair, Sustainability for the Twenty-First Century. One of the members has prepared a report of background information that will be used to kick off the planning session. You have been asked to organize the document to make it more accessible for the reader. In this exercise, you will create a table of contents and an index and insert headers and footers.

1. Open **W8-R3-WikiSustain** from your **Word Chapter 8** folder and save it as **W8-R3-WikiSustainRevised**.

2. If necessary, display formatting marks; then scroll through the document and observe the heading styles.

   Now you will insert a new page for the table of contents and then generate the table of contents.

3. On the second page, position the insertion point in front of *Introduction*.

4. Choose **Layout→Page Setup→Breaks** and insert a **Next Page** section break.

5. Scroll up and position the insertion point in front of the section break (to the right of the paragraph symbol) and then tap `Enter`.

6. Choose **References→Table of Contents→Table of Contents** →**Automatic Table 2**.

Update the Table of Contents

7. Hover the mouse pointer over the *Energy* link in the table of contents and then press `Ctrl` and click the link to jump to that heading in the document.

8. Position the insertion point at the end of the *Energy* heading, tap `Spacebar`, and then type **consumption**.

9. Now update the entire table of contents.

Notice that the table of contents updated with the change. Now you'll change the table of contents format.

10. Choose **References→Table of Contents→Table of Contents→Custom Table of Contents**, choose the **Formal** format, click **OK**, and then choose **Yes** to replace the table of contents.

Add Headers and Footers

11. Scroll down and position the insertion point in **section 2**, which begins with *Introduction*.

12. Choose **Insert→Header & Footer→Header** ▢ **→Edit Header** and break the link between sections 1 and 2.

13. Tap ⏭Tab twice to position the insertion point at the right side of the header area, type **Sustainability in the Twenty-First Century**, and close the header area.

Notice that the header appears throughout section 2, but it does not appear in section 1.

14. Position the insertion point in **section 2**; choose **Insert→Header & Footer→Footer** ▢ **→ Edit Footer** and then break the link.

15. Choose **Header & Footer Tools→Design→Header & Footer→Footer** ▢ **→Austin**.

Now you will set the page numbering to start at 1 in section 2.

16. Choose **Header & Footer Tools→Design→Header & Footer→Page Number** ▢ and then choose **Format Page Numbers**.

17. Set the numbering to start at 1 and then close the footer area.

Create an Index

18. Select the *Atmosphere* heading toward the top of the new page 1 and mark it as an index entry.

19. Type **global warming** in the Subentry field and then click **Mark**.

20. Select the text in the Subentry field, type **carbon reduction** in its place, and click Mark.

21. Select the Subentry text, type **air pollution:nitrogen oxides** (no spaces surrounding the colon), and click **Mark**.

Whether you're creating a concordance or marking entries in the Mark Index Entry dialog box, the word to the right of the colon is a subentry of the word on the left.

22. Now mark these items in the Subentry field:
    ```
    air pollution:sulfur oxides
    air pollution:photochemical smog
    air pollution:acid rain
    air pollution:sulfate aerosols
    ```

23. Click in the document, scroll down and select *Management of human consumption* toward the bottom of page 2, and then click the dialog box to activate it.

24. Type **Energy Consumption:increase in CO2** in the Subentry field and click **Mark**.

25. Mark these entries in the Subentry field:

```
Energy Consumption:fossil fuel emissions
Energy Consumption:climate change
harvesting rainwater
ethical consumerism
local food production
circular material flow
renewable sources
industrial ecology
```

26. Close the dialog box.

27. Position the insertion point at the end of the document, create a new page for the index, and then turn off formatting marks.

   Remember, the index codes can cause a change in pagination.

28. Type **Index** and tap Enter, format the text with **bold**, **14 pt**, and then position the insertion point on the blank line below the text.

29. Insert an index using the Modern format, right-align page numbers, and use dots as the tab leader.

   Notice the subentries under air pollution *and* Energy Consumption. *Now you'll mark another entry and then update the index.*

30. Scroll to page 1, select the *Freshwater and oceans* heading, and mark it as an index entry.

31. Click in the document, select the *Land use* heading on page 2, mark it as an index entry, and then close the Mark Index Entry dialog box.

32. Turn off formatting marks.

   Word turned on formatting marks when you marked the new index entries.

33. Position the insertion point in the index and tap F9.

Keep Text Together

If this document is revised, using some pagination features will simplify the process. In this example, you want the Management of human consumption *heading to always be at the top of a new page.*

34. Scroll to page 2 and position the insertion point in front of *Management of human consumption.*

35. Choose **Home→Paragraph→dialog box launcher** ⌐ and, if necessary, click the **Line and Page Breaks** tab.

   Some pagination options are already in place for this text.

36. Check the **Page Break Before** checkbox and click **OK**.

   This ensures that this heading will always start on a new page. Because pagination has changed, it's a good idea to update the table of contents and the index.

37. Position the insertion point in the table of contents and update the entire table.

38. Position the insertion point in the index and tap F9.

39. Save and close the document.

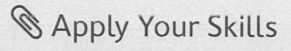 # Apply Your Skills

APPLY YOUR SKILLS: W8-A1

Finalize a Report

Universal Corporate Events sent you to Munich on a familiarization trip. You have completed the content for your report and now will apply some formatting. In this exercise, you will create a table of contents to make it easy to locate specific topics in the report and also add a header and footer.

1. Open **W8-A1-Munich** from your **Word Chapter 8** folder and save it as **W8-A1-MunichRevised**.

2. Open the **Styles** task pane, scroll through the document to observe some of the heading styles in use, and then close the task pane.

3. Position the insertion point in front of *Introduction* on the first page of the body and insert a **Next Page** section break.

4. If necessary, display formatting marks, scroll up and position the insertion point in front of the section break, and tap Enter.

5. Insert an **Automatic Table 1** table of contents and use the **Parks** hyperlink to jump to that heading.

6. Position the insertion point at the end of the heading, tap Spacebar, and type **and recreation**.

7. Update the table of contents to reflect the change.

8. Open the Table of Contents dialog box, apply the **Classic** format, choose the **dots** from the Tab Leader drop-down list, and click **OK**.

9. When the message box appears confirming the replacement, click **OK**.

10. Position the insertion point in **section 2**, which begins with *Introduction*, edit the header, and break the link between sections 1 and 2.

11. Insert a header using the **Banded** style from the Header gallery; close the header area.

12. With the insertion point in section 2, edit the footer to break the link between sections 1 and 2, and then insert a footer using the Banded style.

13. Set up the page numbering to start at **1** in section 2.

14. Close the footer area and then save and close the document.

APPLY YOUR SKILLS: W8-A2

Create an Index and Use Pagination Options

Universal Corporate Events has asked you to do some research on Bangalore for a client. Now that you've completed the research, you will add an index making it easy for the client to locate important terms. In this exercise, you will mark entries and subentries and use a concordance to create the index. Then you will make additions to the index and update it.

1. Open **W8-A2-Bangalore** from your **Word Chapter 8** folder and save it as **W8-A2-BangaloreRevised**.

2. If necessary, display formatting marks; then mark the three main headings on page 1 (*Background*, *Climate*, and *Get in*) as main index entries.

3. Mark *By plane* as a subentry of *Get in*.

4. On page 6, mark *Landmarks* and *Temples* as main index entries.

5. Navigate to your **Word Chapter 8** folder and open **W8-A2-Concordance**, examine the file, and then close it.

6. Use the **AutoMark** button in the Index dialog box, together with **W8-A2-Concordance**, to mark additional index entries and then turn off formatting marks.

   Now you'll insert an index.

7. Scroll to the end of the document and insert a page break to create a blank page for your index.

8. Type **Index** at the top of the new, blank page and tap ⏎Enter.

9. Format *Index* with **bold, 14 pt**, position the insertion point on the blank line below the heading, and insert an index using the **Formal** format.

10. Scroll up to page 1 and select *Background*.

11. Choose **References→Index→Mark Entry**.

12. Mark these terms as subentries of Background:
    - population
    - Garden City of India
    - IT industry

13. Turn off formatting marks and update the index.

14. On page 1, select the *Background* heading.

15. Open the Paragraph dialog box and check **Keep with Next** on the Line and Page Breaks tab.

16. Select the *Climate* heading and apply the **Keep with Next** option.

17. Select the *Get in* and *By plane* headings and apply the **Keep with Next** option.

18. Save and close the file.

APPLY YOUR SKILLS: W8-A3

Organize a Long Document

A Universal Corporate Events agent wrote a report on Basque country. Now it's time to enhance the document's readability. In this exercise, you will create a table of contents and an index. You will work with headers and footers and set up a page break pagination option.

1. Open **W8-A3-Basque** from your **Word Chapter 8** folder and save it as **W8-A3-BasqueRevised**.

2. If necessary, display formatting marks; then open the **Styles** task pane.

3. Scroll through the document, observe the heading styles, and then close the task pane.

4. To create a new page for the table of contents, insert a **Next Page** section break just before the heading *The Basque Country* on page 2.

5. Scroll up, position the insertion point in front of the section break, tap ⏎Enter, and then insert an **Automatic Table 2** table of contents.

6. Use the **Climate** link in the table of contents to jump to the *Climate* heading; type **Basque** in front of *Climate* and then update the table of contents to reflect the change.

7. Create a custom table of contents by applying the **Distinctive** format.

8. Position the insertion point in section 2, which begins with *The Basque Country* heading; edit the header, break the link between sections 1 and 2, and insert a header using the **Blank style**.

9. Type **The Basque Country** in the Type Here area; close the header area.

10. With the insertion point in section 2, edit the footer and break the link between sections 1 and 2.

11. Insert a footer using the **Austin style** and format the starting page number to start at page 1; close the footer area.

Mark Entries and Create an Index

12. Mark index main entries and subentries using the headings indicated in this table.

Main Entry	Subentry
Features	Atlantic Basin Middle section Ebro Valley
Basque Climate	
Transport	Road Rail Airports Seaports

13. Turn off formatting marks, position the insertion point at the end of the document, and insert a page break.

14. Type **Index** and tap ⟦Enter⟧, format the text with **bold, 14 pt**, position the insertion point on the blank line below the heading, and insert a **Formal** index.

15. Mark the *Cuisine* heading (page 4) as a main entry, turn off formatting marks, and then update the index.

Keep Text Together

16. Position the insertion point in front of the *Transport* heading (page 2) and insert the **Page Break Before** pagination option.

17. Because you changed pagination, update the table of contents and the index.

18. Save and close the file.

◢ Extend Your Skills

These exercises challenge you to think critically and apply your new skills. You will be evaluated on your ability to follow directions, completeness, creativity, and the use of proper grammar and mechanics. Save files to your chapter folder. Submit assignments as directed.

W8-E1 That's the Way I See It

As a small-business owner, you want to offer your customers a document that provides an in-depth, categorized overview of your products. If you were a bookstore owner, for example, you might categorize books by genre (e.g., history, biography, fiction). Start a new document and save it as **W8-E1-ProductDescriptions**. Decide on the type and name of your business. Type an introduction (3–4 sentences) for each main product category, providing longer content for the subcategories. Format main categories with Heading 1 and give each at least three subcategories (Heading 2). Your document should be at least seven pages, including a cover page, a table of contents, and index (ten main entries and at least three subentries). Be sure to insert a Next Page section break between the table of contents and the body of the document. Also include multiple footers (page numbering starting at page 1 in section 2, no footers in section 1) and the Keep Text Together option (keep heading lines together with the paragraph following headings; apply this feature at least twice). You may copy content from the Internet, but cite your sources.

W8-E2 Be Your Own Boss

As the owner of Blue Jean Landscaping, you want to provide your customers with in-depth information for their spring gardens, focusing on fruits, vegetables, and legumes. Start a new document and save it as **W8-E2-SpringPlanting**. Create an introduction (3–4 sentences). Do online research to create at least three subcategories for each category. Format the category headings with Heading 1 and the subcategories with Heading 2. Provide detailed information, such as the best growing conditions for a particular type of tomato. Your document should be at least seven pages, with a cover page, table of contents, and index. You may copy content from the Internet, but cite your sources. Insert a Next Page section break between the table of contents and the document body. Use page numbers in the section 2 footer, starting at page 1; use no footer in section 1. Your index should include twenty main entries and at least five subentries.

W8-E3 Demonstrate Proficiency

Stormy BBQ is planning to sell a book about BBQ cooking, and you have been asked to provide the research, which you will do online. You can feel free to copy content from online sources—just remember to cite your sources. Start a new document and save it as **W8-E3-BBQBook**. The book will include three main categories: BBQ Grills and Tools, BBQ Tips and Techniques, and BBQ Recipes. Each category heading should be formatted with the Heading 1 style. Create a short introduction (3–4 sentences) for each main category. Based on your research identify at least two subcategories for each category; format the subcategory headings with the Heading 2 style. Use a Next Page section break to designate a cover page and table of contents as section 1 and the rest of the document as section 2. Insert a header with the company name that appears only in section 2. Insert a page number footer that appears only in section 2 and that starts numbering at page 1. Create an index of at least fifteen terms of your choice, including main entries and at least five subentries.

Glossary

bookmark Selection of text or other objects identified by a name and location; enables quick navigation through long documents

concordance A list of terms used to mark words or phrases in a document that are to be included in an index

data source In Mail Merge, the variable data that merges with the main document; controlled by merge fields in the main document

Mail Merge Feature used to personalize standard letters, envelopes, mailing labels, and other documents by combining a main document with a data source

main document In a Mail Merge, the document that contains the content that remains the same for each recipient; controls the merge with merge fields

merge fields Placeholders in a Mail Merge main document that instruct Word to insert information from a data source

merged document Document that results when you complete a merge of the main document and the data source

nonbreaking spaces or hyphens Spaces or hyphens inserted between two or more words to keep those words together on the same line

style sets Used to change font and paragraph properties, interact with themes; most effective when used in conjunction with Styles gallery

watermark Text or images placed in the header of a document so it appears faintly behind document text and graphics

Widow/Orphan control Prevents placing the last line of a paragraph at the top of the next page (widow) or the first line of a paragraph at the bottom of a page (orphan); ensures there are at least two lines of a paragraph at the top or bottom of a page

Index

Note: Page numbers ending with a "V" indicate that a term is discussed in the video referenced on that page.

NOTES

NOTES

NOTES

NOTES

NOTES

NOTES

NOTES

NOTES